THE
IMMUTABLE
LAW
— OF THE —
SEED

Experience the
Resources of Heaven

DR. JIM RICHARDS

Copyright © 2024 Dr. Jim Richards All rights reserved.

No part of this publication may be reproduced, stored, or transmitted in any form or by any means, including written, copied, or electronically, without prior written permission from the author or his agents. The only exception is brief quotations in printed reviews. Short excerpts may be used with the publisher's or author's expressed written permission.

All Scripture quotations, unless otherwise noted, are from the New King James Version of the Bible. Copyright © 1982 by Thomas Nelson, Inc. Used by permission. All rights reserved.

The Immutable Law of the Seed: Experience the Resources of Heaven

Cover and Interior Page design by True Potential, Inc.

ISBN: (Paperback): 9781960024572

ISBN: (e-book): 9781960024589

LCCN: 2024949529

True Potential, Inc.
PO Box 904, Travelers Rest, SC 29690
www.truepotentialmedia.com
Cover and Interior Page design by True Potential, Inc.

Contents

1. Making This Work — 5
2. A Different Kind Of Faith — 11
3. God of Order — 15
4. The God of Creation — 21
5. Immutable Laws — 25
6. Worn Down By The World — 31
7. The God of Yes — 37
8. The Subconscious Filter — 43
9. Habits or Choices — 51
   Section II: The Sower and The Seed — 57
10. The Sower — 59
11. The Propagation of The Seed — 65
12. The Wayside — 71
13. Seeds on Stony Ground — 77
14. Seeds Among Thorns — 83
15. Seeds In Good Soil — 89
16. Be Careful What you hear — 95
17. The Multiplication Factor — 99
18. The Measure You Meet — 103
19. Harmony With God — 109

20. We Are What We Digest	117
21. Faith And Patience	121
22. Ears To Hear	127
23. Discerning The Voice of God	133
24. A Teachable Heart	141
25. Opening Your Understanding	147
26. Activating The Seed	151
27. Watching Over The Seed	157
28. Finding The Treasure	165
29. Everything is Made New	171
30. A Way of Life	177

1. Making This Work

All our beliefs are just theories until we get them to work!

The Immutable Law of the Seed applies to every area of our lives. It happens whether we have faith or not, whether we want the outcome, or whether we pray and believe for something else to happen. *The Immutable Law of the Seed* is programmed into the Physics of Creation! Without it the universe could not continue to exist!

For those who hear and understand the *Immutable Law of the Seed*, faith becomes incredibly simple. For those who ignore it and attempt to operate faith based on religious traditions, there will always be frustration, disappointment, and inconsistent outcomes when attempting to walk in faith.

This book is based on Jesus' teachings about the Sower and the Seed. His teachings about this are primarily focused on the way this affects our capacity to live and function in the Kingdom of Heaven!

According to reliable sources, the Kingdom of God and the Kingdom of Heaven are not synonymous, although the majority of teachers and preachers teach that it is. However, as a literalist, I choose to recognize God's choice of words. I think every word is important enough for us to accurately understand its meaning. The ancients believed that every letter of every word and every jot or tittle was important to the meaning of words. They believe that when the Messiah comes, we will understand every aspect of the entire Word of God!

I accept the entire Bible as God's inspired word. There are, however, considerations. The first five books of the Bible were given to Moses in complete and perfect form. They are God speaking directly. All Scripture is based on the Torah, the first five books of the Bible! Jesus' teachings are the Word of God based on God's motives and intentions. He perfectly represented God in everything He did and taught! All the rest of the books were written by men who were inspired by the Holy Spirit.

If my appraisal of the Scriptures is correct, the portions of the Scripture that we should master in order to understand all the rest of the Scriptures are the Torah and Jesus' teaching.

I don't think there are synonyms in the Bible. There are words that are similar, but they are not synonyms. Words that are similar reveal different aspects or dimensions of the topic to which they refer. They reveal different nuances of truth. When we consider words to be synonyms, we lose the capacity to see many of the subtle nuances of God's Word.

JESUS IS THE LIVING WORD. HE MUST BE THE BASIS FOR INTERPRETING AND APPLYING SCRIPTURE.

The Lordship of Jesus is expressed in the written Word. But Jesus' life, ministry, teachings, sacrifice, and Covenant reveal how to understand and apply the Word from God's original intentions and motive. Jesus is the Living Word. He must be the basis for interpreting and applying Scripture.

We can be no more submitted to His Lordship than we are to His interpretation of the Word. Jesus was very clear about this. To call Him Lord and then place other portions of the Scripture above His teachings is, on a practical level, a denial of His Lordship. Look at His own words.

> *Therefore whoever **hears** these sayings of Mine, and **does** them, I will liken him to a **wise man** who built his house on the rock: and the rain descended, the floods came, and the winds blew and beat on **that house**, and it **did not fall**, for it was founded on the rock.*

MAKING THIS WORK

> *But everyone who **hears** these sayings of Mine, and **does not do them**, will be like **a foolish man** who built his house on the sand: and the rain descended, the floods came, and the winds blew and beat on **that house**; and it **fell**. **And great was its fall**."*
> (Matthew 7:24-27)

In the English translation, Jesus refers to His teachings as "His sayings." The word "sayings" comes from the Greek word "logos." Jesus, as the Logos, revealed God's way, logic, wisdom, character, motive, and intention as it looks when put into practice.

I often emphasize this in my writings, but it bears repeating: from the moment sin was introduced, no human on Earth fully grasped God's character, motives, and intentions. Jesus is the only person who has ever dwelt on Earth who properly interpreted and applied the Word of God. Contemplating His life, teachings, ministry, death, burial, resurrection, and the Covenant God established with Him is the beginning of understanding.

If Jesus is not our focal point for all interpretation, we will never grasp the word of the Kingdom; we will never understand the messages in the parables, and we will never see God in the Scriptures as He truly is.

To understand the Parables of the Kingdom, we must first understand the word of the Kingdom. The word "kingdom" comes from the Greek word "basileía," which refers to a royal dominion.[1] The Kingdom of God is about Jesus' rule. We enter into it at the new birth based on our commitment to Jesus' Lordship. We are not ready to enter the Kingdom of Heaven until we have settled the issue of Lordship.

Many believe that the Kingdom of Heaven refers to our abode after we die. However, the Kingdom of Heaven is the realm we enter where we participate in the provision of heaven here on Earth.

There are three dimensions of the Kingdom of Heaven. The first is the realm we enter into in our hearts, now in this life. The parables of the *Immutable Law of the Seed* are all about establishing and experiencing this realm. The second manifestation of the Kingdom of Heaven will occur when Jesus returns to Earth and sets up His Kingdom for a thousand

---

[1] The Complete Word Study Dictionary: New Testament © 1992 by AMG International, Inc. Revised Edition, 1993

years. The final expression of the Kingdom of Heaven will be when the New Jerusalem descends from above. It is in this dimension that we will enjoy the fullness of God's resources.

Under the Old Covenant, one of the most celebrated offerings or feasts was the Peace Offering. When a person lost confidence in their standing before God due to their thoughts and actions, they could bring a sin offering. Or, if they simply felt disconnected from God, they could bring a "draw near" offering.

In fact, all sacrifices were "draw near" offerings. The Old Covenant wasn't based on fear and legalism, as many suggest. None of the sacrifices were designed to move God or compel Him in any way. They were acts of faith. He promised the Israelites that He would never leave them or forsake them. Faith believes that promise! When done in faith, trusting in His promise to be there and restore fellowship, every sacrifice was an action that affected the heart of the worshiper, drawing them near to God in their hearts. It didn't cause God to change His heart.

When they gave their offering and believed it was received, they would enter into peace. Then, they would offer a Peace Offering. This was not an offering to obtain peace; it was a celebration of the peace of God that replaced guilt and condemnation.

What made this offering so celebrated was that when they felt peace, they knew they once again had access to all the resources of heaven.

Our Heavenly Father is the God of Peace; Jesus is the Prince of Peace. He established the Covenant of Peace with God (Isaiah 54:10). The message of the Gospel is the *Gospel of Peace*. Scripture tells us to let peace rule in our hearts. When we believe the Gospel, what happened on the Cross, in the grave, and through the resurrection, we experience a peace that surpasses all understanding. It is in this place of peace, surrendered to the Lordship of Jesus, confident in His finished work, and experiencing resurrection life that we can recognize and share in the resources of the Kingdom of Heaven.

The peace of God in our hearts creates a continuum of peace. Perceiving the resources of Heaven gives us even more peace. Based on the *Immutable Law of the Seed*, we receive more of what we already have. Having peace in our hearts makes us capable of perceiving access to His resources, which causes us to abound more and more in the peace of God.

The parables of the Kingdom are not about going to heaven after we die. They are not about earning anything from God. They present the principles by which a disciple lives life and relates to others. They are snapshots of what we look like as we express the Logos of God.

Based on Jesus' teaching, the *Immutable Law of the Seed* is the way we bear the fruit of righteousness and live by the values and principles that maintain peace in our hearts and peace in the Kingdom.

> # THE LAW OF THE SEED IS IMMUTABLE—UNCHANGEABLE!

The *Law of the Seed* is immutable—unchangeable! It doesn't matter what our opinion might be; it doesn't matter what seems reasonable to us. It works the way Jesus said. It is the non-legalistic way to plant and nurture the Word of God in hearts that produce the fruit of a Kingdom life!

Making This Work

Studying the Word without applying it to our life is meaningless. It is simply the gathering of information. At the end of each chapter, there are brief instructions. The exercises are incredibly simple but unbelievably powerful. You'll be applying the principles of "Meditative Bible" reading.

The ancients have a saying: There are fifty faces to the Torah.[2] This means there are dozens of ways we can study and interpret the Scripture. Each method adds greater depth to our insight into God's Word.

After our due diligence to translate and interpret the Word, the last and most important step in the process is to invite God into this encounter. This is the prayer we should pray every time we read the Scripture. We will apply this to every chapter of this book.

"Based on what I'm seeing in each chapter, the most important question is this, "Father, in light of what I'm seeing in this chapter, what are you saying to me, and how will I apply this to my life?"

---

2   Chaim Bentorah

Then, wait before the Lord. This exercise will expand your capacity to hear and follow God!

Make notes of everything He reveals to you and every way you see how you can apply the truth that is speaking to your heart!

This is the very first step toward planting the seed in your heart. The Word God speaks into your heart is a Divine prescription for how you get the greatest benefit from anything you hear, see, or think!

Divine Prescriptions

In the Hebrew language, the instructions, corrections, and warnings in God's Word are considered Divine Prescriptions. Prescriptions tend to both prevent illness and cure it. Identify the prescriptions God gave you as you read this chapter.

- Take time to ponder what God spoke to you in this chapter.
- Ask Him, "In light of what I'm seeing, what are you speaking to me?"
- Then, "How do I apply what I'm seeing to my life?"
- Regardless of How I personally feel about what you're showing me, "You are my Lord. I am willing to follow your leadership."
- I am willing for you to bring me to the place of trusting and applying everything you speak to me."

2. A Different Kind Of Faith

Trust is based on faithfulness; therefore, our faith is rooted in the degree to which we consider God faithful!

It seems, for the most part, that when believers talk about faith, it is either faith for salvation or faith to receive a particular benefit from God. Both of these aspects of faith are important. However, it seems we may be missing out on the larger concept of faith. By using our faith for individual needs, we tend to go from crisis to crisis, using our faith as a reaction to circumstances. We could, however, expand the use of faith for a more proactive life.

There is a much more effective way to walk in faith. Instead of operating faith one issue at a time, there is a more comprehensive way to walk in faith. When our faith is in who God is—His character, we can operate faith in a way that covers all of our life's needs and dreams.

The name Jehovah-Jireh is well-known among almost every believer. It Is commonly translated as Jehovah will provide. According to some Hebrew scholars, that is only a portion of what that name means. When we look at the patterns of God's provision and protection throughout history, we see that He has anticipated and made provision for every need before it occurs.

The Immutable Law of the Seed

According to some sources, a fuller translation of Jehovah-Jireh is "Jehovah sees and provides."[3] While examples of this are all throughout the Scriptures, the clearest place to see this is when God told Abraham to sacrifice Isaac. As we all know, God had no intention of allowing Abraham to sacrifice his son. But what God needed Abraham to see was that Jehovah sees in advance and is already there with a solution before we realize the need!

When God called out to Abraham not to harm Isaac, he turned and saw a ram caught in a thicket. Based on that, he named the place *"The Lord will see and provide."* (Genesis 22:14)

> **THE MOST DRAMATIC EXAMPLE OF GOD SEEING THE NEED IN ADVANCE IS WHAT HE DID FOR OUR SALVATION.**

The Most dramatic example of God seeing the need in advance is what He did for our salvation. Before He created the world, before He created man, before man succumbed to temptation, God had already anticipated the need for a Savior (Ephesians 1:4).

If we know that, before the foundations of the world, God has always seen every need we will face and has proactively provided to meet that need, it becomes a game changer. Now, our faith is in God's character. Instead of living from individual crisis to crisis, we could live from glory to glory!

It seems we use faith as if God needs a reminder of our situation before He will take action. In fact, many believers think faith is where we persuade God to take action! When we know God saw our situation in advance and provided for it, we no longer have to enter into "fight-or-flight" mode. We simply rest in the confidence that God answered before we call (Isaiah 65:24). This is a place of continual rest!

So often, as we "walk out our beliefs," we discover dimensions of reality that were never considered at the beginning of our journey. This doesn't mean we were wrong; it just means that we are seeing greater dimensions of a particular truth! This is the case with our understanding and appli-

---
3   (Biblesoft's New Exhaustive Strong's Numbers and Concordance with Expanded Greek-Hebrew Dictionary. Copyright © 1994, 2003, 2006, 2010 Biblesoft, Inc. and International Bible Translators, Inc.)

cation of faith. Over the past one hundred years, the concept of faith has grown from trusting God for salvation to believing for miracles to trusting God for individual promises.

It's not that our early concepts of "faith" were wrong. They are still valuable for daily life. However, we now understand that every aspect of faith stands on the foundation of God's character. All the nuances of faith have their roots in His faithfulness! As we explore a broader concept of faith, we will realize a simpler, more positive dimension of the faith walk.

God's promises are an expression of His love. His desire to meet our needs is an expression of His compassion. But this is where we jump beyond the finite mind to eternal reality. The fact that He has already prepared to meet our needs before we see them and before we pray about them is the heart of His faithfulness.

His faithfulness to keep His promises is a merciful expression of His love. After all, we don't escape the destruction of the world's system by grit and willpower. We escape by trusting and receiving His precious promises. Promises were made in the past because God anticipated our every need.

> *Which have been given to us exceedingly great and precious **promises**, that through these you may be partakers of the **divine nature**, having **escaped the corruption** that is in the world through lust.* (2 Peter 1:4)

When we believe that He is who He says He is, i.e., the one who sees and provides, it influences our heart, making us able to see His provision. Most of our "praying" and begging God to meet our needs is because we can't perceive His provision.

Here is the mystery of God's faithfulness. Since He **has already given** us all things that pertain to life and godliness (2 Peter 1:3), he doesn't have to make a decision or take action to meet our needs. It was settled in heaven.

As we realize God is faithful, our confidence in Him reaches new heights. We no longer think of Him as a "stranger" that we hope will keep His promises. This is someone we know! We know His ways; our faith is based on who He is and what He **has done**; therefore, we know what to expect from Him.

This is a different kind of faith. This supersedes the intellectual boundaries of our finite mind! It includes much of what we have been taught about faith but takes it into greater dimensions.

The fact that God made all these things available to us before Creation and the fact that He programmed many of His promises into the fabric of creation challenges us to enter into a new kind of Faith.

Divine Prescriptions

In the Hebrew language, the instructions, corrections, and warnings in God's Word are considered Divine Prescriptions. Prescriptions tend to both prevent illness and cure it. Identify the prescriptions God gave you as you read this chapter.

- Take time to ponder what God spoke to you in this chapter.
- Ask Him, "In light of what I'm seeing, what are you speaking to me?"
- Then, "How do I apply what I'm seeing to my life?"
- Regardless of How I personally feel about what you're showing me, "You are my Lord. I am willing to follow your leadership."
- I am willing for you to bring me to the place of trusting and applying everything you speak to me."

3. God of Order

When God's absolutes are ignored, chaos and confusion rule!

Our God is a God of order, not chaos (1 Corinthians 14:33). To have order, there must be laws, and those laws must be absolute. When there are no absolutes, chaos reigns. Because of the influence of false science, we have come to believe that all things in creation came about randomly.

Randomness produces uncertainty, but predictable laws provide a sense of certainty, order, and predictability. In a complex environment, laws must be capable of coordinating and synchronizing millions and millions of bits of information with incredible precision, beyond anything possible by the greatest supercomputers. There can be degrees of randomness within certain events, but there can be no uncertainty concerning the laws that regulate harmony between all the factors and functions!

It is imperative that we understand that the consciousness of laws has nothing to do with religious legalism. The observance of laws is not a measurement of spirituality; it is actually the fruit of wisdom. The wise seek to know and understand the laws that govern an entity or environment and work in harmony with those laws. To launch into any endeavor without understanding the laws that govern the situation is an act of reckless foolishness!

Many researchers agree that after the division of languages at the Tower of Babel, the Chinese and those who became the Nation of Israel seemed to retain more of their knowledge handed down from the beginning of the human race. Their science, medical practices, and even many of their religious beliefs were more in harmony with the Word of God than any group other than the Hebrews. Even their mode of writing was similar to the original Hebrew, and they share some of the same pictographs.

The Chinese operated by an immutable principle called the *Tao* (pronounced Dao). The *Tao* is the Chinese equivalent of the Greek word *Logos*, which describes very specific aspects of Jesus' life, mission, and ministry! Our understanding of the *Tao* has been clouded by the religious paganism that eventually developed around the concept. But be assured, there is no correlation between the original meaning of the *Tao* and the way the word is used today.

> TAO HAS AN ALMOST EXACT MEANING AS THE WORD LOGOS, WHICH DESCRIBES WHAT JESUS CAME TO PRESENT HERE ON PLANET EARTH!

Tao has an almost exact meaning as the word *Logos*, which describes what Jesus came to present here on planet Earth! Both the *Tao* and the *Logos* could loosely mean "the way." It is used in the Chinese New Testament in the same places the Greek uses the word *logos* as a reference to Jesus. The ancient Chinese believed in God, i.e., the same God as that of the Hebrews. Originally, their medicine, science, and religious beliefs were very similar to those who followed the knowledge of God. They knew things about the universe, our solar system, and human life that couldn't have been possible apart from God.

When they spoke of the *Tao,* they were talking about a specific logic. The *Tao* was "the way" things flow in the created world! They knew there was a Creator; they knew He had created the world around an organized logic, i.e., the way things should go! They realized that the ease of success in any endeavor was dependent on how well they understood the laws that regulated life and their willingness to harmonize with those laws instead of attempting to force them to change! As people of faith, we don't attempt to make the laws work. If we believe they work because God created them to do so, we use our faith to harmonize with the way God created the world. This is precisely what Jesus meant when He said, *"Take My yoke upon you and learn from Me, for I am gentle and lowly in heart, and you will find rest for your souls. For My yoke is easy and My burden is light."* (Matthew 11:29-30)

Yielding to the *Logos* (Jesus the Creator) and His ways not only renders a good outcome but, as an added bonus, the way is easy and light! We, as believers, would do well to understand the laws by which God created all things and learn how to work with those laws.

Our concept of faith today has come to subtly differ from that originally found in Scripture. The Scripture tells us about a path we can walk that is easy, filled with life, and absolutely no death (Proverbs 12:28). But our tendency is to walk in our own path instead of His path. Then, when the way gets hard, we use what we believe to be faith to get God to deliver us from the consequences of the path we have chosen. So rather than working with the *Logos,* the way, and the wisdom of God, we work against it and think we can change the consequences.

One of the things about which believers seem to be deeply confused is Jesus' role in creation. This confusion lends itself to many of our misunderstandings of faith. Consider the following verses:

- **Ephesians 3:9**: *"The mystery, which from the beginning of the ages has been hidden in God who created all things **through Jesus Christ**."*
    - o There are mysteries that have been hidden from the beginning, which God seeks to make known to His church. It seems many of these mysteries are linked to the role Jesus played in creation.

- **Colossians 1:16-18**: *"For **by Him all things were created** that are in heaven and that are on earth, visible and invisible, whether thrones or dominions or principalities or powers. All things were created through Him and for Him. And He is before all things, and in Him all things consist."*
    - o Grasping our victory over all principalities and powers is intimately linked to Jesus' preeminence in creation.

- **Hebrews 1:1-3**: *"God, who at various times and in various ways spoke in time past to the fathers by the prophets, has in these last days spoken* *to us by His Son, whom He has appointed heir of all things, **through whom also He made the worlds**; who being the brightness of His glory and the express image of His person, and **upholding** all things **by the word of His power**..."*

- o All the created world maintains its order through His spoken word and the wisdom and power behind that Word.

Everything about Jesus was a revelation of God's *Logos*! He, personally, is the *Logos*. But His way is also the way of the *Logos*. He never does anything that denies or contradicts God's wisdom. When we observe Him, we perceive the logic, wisdom, character, and nature of the Father. Likewise, all His works were in harmony with the *Logos*. With Him, there is no variableness nor shadow of turning (James 1:17).

He is the basis for us to understand God. By Him and His actions, we can know what to expect from God. He is the way, i.e., the way things were designed to work. He is the truth; He is the only exact representation of God to the world! But most interesting is the fact that, as the *Logos*, He is the life of God manifest on planet Earth! All confusion about God ends when we look at Jesus as the *Logos*, i.e., the living, breathing manifestation of all God is!

When we look at creation, we see some of the eternal laws of God. It is in creation that we see the first glimpse of the Immutable *Law of the Seed*! The *Law of the Seed* is one of the most important laws we must grasp for a faith that's easy and light! This will unlock the mysteries of faith. It will put an end to life always being hard. It will also untangle many of the conflicting beliefs about God that make it nearly impossible to know Him intimately!

God (Father/Son/Holy Spirit) modeled the *Law of the Seed* in every aspect of creation. At the end of each creation process, God would inspect His work to determine if it was in perfect harmony with His will for the human race. He was, after all, creating a habitat designed to sustain human life at the highest possible level.

Each time He examined His work, He saw that it was "good." Chaim Bentorah, in his book *Learning God's Love Language*,[4] points out that the

---
[4] https://www.truepotentialmedia.com/product/learning-gods-love-language-book-workbook-bundle/

Hebrew word translated as "good" always implies harmony. Obviously, the word *good* tells us His creation was pleasant, enjoyable, and to be desired. But in the fact that it always means harmony, we realize the reason it was good was because it was in harmony with God's character, which was in harmony with His intentions.

Jesus said, *"Even so, every good tree bears good fruit, but a bad tree bears bad fruit."* (Matthew 7:17) Our words and deeds are fruit. Fruit grows from a seed. We may all do the occasional good deed, but fruit represents that which is habitual. It is a way (*Logos*) of our lives. It is the path we have chosen!

Our first life lesson from the *Law of the Seed* is this: our words and deeds are an expression of the seed that is in our hearts. To live one way and profess that our character is another is a denial of the *Law of the Seed*! According to the Apostle John, it is also an indication of darkness (self-deception) in our hearts.

The fruit of God's character was to create a world that was perfect in every way. The world was created in a way that would have sustained physical life forever, with no death, disease, or lack—until sin was introduced.

Divine Prescriptions

The key to a life full of good fruit is to ensure the seed we are planting is the proper seed that will produce the desired outcome. Every page in this book will unfold the subtle mysteries of the *Immutable Law of the Seed*.

- Take time to ponder what God spoke to you in this chapter.
- Ask Him, "In light of what I'm seeing, what are you speaking to me?"
- Then, "How do I apply what I'm seeing to my life?"
- Regardless of how I personally feel about what You're showing me, "You are my Lord. I am willing to follow Your leadership."
- I am willing for You to bring me to the place of trusting and applying everything You speak to me."

4. The God of Creation

When we perceive the glory of the creation, we perceive the invisible attributes of the Creator!

In the previous chapter, we uncovered what we all knew at some deep level: "I can know God's character by His promises, His words, and His actions." In this chapter, we will weave another strand into this cord: creation. We can discover incredible insights about God through His creation! In fact, Paul says we can understand the invisible attributes of God through His creation. However, for this to occur, we must believe His account of creation.

Fortunately, we live in a time when there is a mountain of scientific evidence to support the biblical account of creation. If we dismiss creation as a myth, we undermine our confidence in the entire Word of God. However, if we only expose ourselves to those who deliberately oppose the biblical account of creation, we undermine our faith. Believing God's account of creation is the first pillar of our faith!

As previously discussed, God's ways cannot be separated from His **deeds**. Everything He does is in harmony with His own character. Deuteronomy 32:4 declares, *"His work is perfect (flawless, complete, righteous, without blemish)."* Again, in Psalm 145:17, the Scripture testifies, *"The Lord is righteous in all His ways."* This tells me that I can expect the same qualities and characteristics in His actions that are present in His character. There is no place where this is clearer than in creation.

The ancients studied the Scripture, looking for patterns. Patterns reveal truth that is not fully revealed through a single verse. But when we see characteristics of God that are present in His name, His actions, His promises, in creation, and in Jesus, we see a pattern. Each of these areas is a witness that comes together to declare an immutable truth about God! This introduces us to a dimension of faith and trust beyond what many believers have ever considered!

Psalm 19:1 is a well-known verse that states, *"The heavens declare the glory of God..."* God is glorified when His characteristics are recognized in a person or event. When Jesus healed the sick and worked miracles, He did it to glorify (reveal) God. This meant that anyone observing would immediately see that the works of Jesus were an exact expression of the character of God and a demonstration of the power of the Spirit of God!

> IN CREATION, WE SEE MANY OF WHAT I CALL, THE FIRST PILLARS OF FAITH.

In creation, we see many of what I call, the first pillars of faith. We see God's motives and intentions revealed in ways that are foundational to everything else we believe about God. In fact, until we believe God's account of creation, we will always struggle with faith and will usually have contradicting views of God, causing massive internal limitations.

We shall now begin to identify and explain the *Immutable Law of the Seed*. This pattern, which is expressed throughout all the Scriptures, is first seen and most clearly modeled in creation. I identify this as one of the most important pillars of faith!

One of the first things we discover about God is an obvious but somewhat obscure concept concerning the *Law of the Seed*: Actions are a fruit! They are effortless, outward manifestations of the seed that is growing in our hearts (Luke 6:44). Creation is the fruit of what God believed and determined in His heart.

Romans 1:20 drives this point home even more clearly, *"For since the creation of the world, His invisible attributes are clearly seen, being understood (comprehended by observance) by the things that are made, even His eternal power and Godhead."*

Modern science is more of a religion aimed at maintaining control of information than an open-minded pursuit of factual knowledge. It tends to start out with an opinion and then interpret the data to support that opinion while ignoring contradictory evidence. As we have witnessed in recent years, "so-called" science has become weaponized by the powerful to control the masses while simultaneously turning people's hearts against God!

There has possibly been more deliberate disinformation concerning creation than any other topic in the Bible. After all, if the biblical account of creation is a myth, then on some level, everything in the Bible becomes a myth. God as Creator is more significant to the understanding of every major biblical doctrine than anything else.

On a side note, the Sabbath is the most regularly celebrated event we are instructed to observe. But why is the Sabbath so important? The Sabbath, among many other things, was to be observed as a day of rest after creation was completed. This should have pointed Hebrew worshipers to acknowledge God as the Creator and reflect on the Genesis account. Instead of it being a day of reflection on God as Creator, the Jews added so many legalistic requirements that it was no longer a celebration of creation but a religious burden, lacking in spiritual significance.

Within creation, God established all the laws of physics. These patterns of creation provide our first "sneak peek" into the *Logos* of God. As we have discovered, Jesus, the *Logos,* created all things in harmony with the wisdom of God. But it has been our failure to comprehend and harmonize with those laws that opened the door to all manner of religious confusion. In this book, we will look at creation to discern what may be the most important and prominent law of creation: *The Immutable Law of the Seed*!

Discovering this law will usher the believer into an entirely new dimension of faith. It will open our understanding of the walk of faith that is easy and light. In fact, it will bring us to what may be the ultimate expression of living in rest while walking in faith!

Each phase of creation was initiated with these words: *"God said."* The Hebrew word for *"said"* means far more than the fact that He spoke. The word tells us that before He spoke, He conceived the outcome in His heart. It also implies that He spoke with intention. We are unable to clearly grasp His intention until He evaluates that aspect of creation to determine if it was good, i.e., pleasing, desirable, and in harmony with His intentions.

His intention was that His creation be in harmony with His desire to create a world that could sustain life indefinitely. Life on Earth would have been a paradise, free from sickness, poverty, toil, and death. And it was… until man chose to bring sin into the equation.

If we discover the *Logos*, i.e., the way of wisdom, in creation, we can harmonize with the Creator. As you will discover, the most important law of creation may well be the *Immutable Law of the Seed*! This law operated when Earth was a paradise, and it operates now in a world that is infested with sin and death.

When I trust the *Law of the Seed*, I trust the Creator. When I have faith in the *Logos* of creation, I have faith in the *Logos* of God.

Divine Prescriptions

- Take time to ponder what God spoke to you in this chapter.
- Ask Him, "In light of what I'm seeing, what are you speaking to me?"
- Then, "How do I apply what I'm seeing to my life?"
- Regardless of how I personally feel about what You're showing me, "You are my Lord. I am willing to follow Your leadership."
- I am willing for You to bring me to a place where I can trust and apply everything You speak to me.

5. Immutable Laws

The finite mind struggles to accept the infinite God!

When something is immutable, it is not subject to change. The laws of physics are believed to be unchanging. Immutability is, however, a somewhat foreign concept to the current generation. Because of their belief in Darwinism, this generation doesn't have a grasp of anything being absolute or unchangeable! They don't even believe humans have always been humans.

Absolute and unchangeable are two factors that, if accepted, would mean that morality and ethics are not fluid; circumstantial morality would not be a consideration. What is right would be right all the time, and what is wrong would be wrong all the time. This helps us understand why so much of the world is so against the God of the Bible. If He is God, He is in charge. Reality is what He says. Morality and ethics are as He defines them. We could no longer determine good and evil for ourselves; therefore, we could not be gods unto ourselves. The majority could not rule; we would understand that just because the majority voted to call something good does not make it good!

To grasp the *Immutable Law of the Seed*, we must first recognize that God is immutable! Let's be sure we understand the concept. Synonyms for immutable would be unchangeable, fixed, unalterable, invariable, determinate, steadfast, inflexible, and not able to be changed, just to name a few!

The Immutable Law of the Seed

We read these Scriptures and somehow fail to make the connection. God never changes who he is and what He does. This means His faithfulness is always predictable!

God cannot and will not change. He is sovereign, i.e., free, autonomous, self-governing, and self-determined. No outside influence can force or entice Him to change.

> **GOD DWELLS OUTSIDE OF TIME. THEREFORE, WHATEVER GOD IS, HE IS THAT FOR ETERNITY.**

God dwells outside of time. Therefore, whatever God is, He is that for eternity. In order for God to change, He would have to exist in the realm of time. When Moses had his first encounter with God, He asked His name, Exodus 3:13. The ancients understood that the "essence" of a deity was initially understood by its name. This is why God is so insistent that we know and believe His names! He uses them to reveal His character and nature!

In Exodus 3:14, God answers Moses, "I AM WHO I AM." An eternal God is who He was, Who He is, and who He shall be. As it says in Malachi 3:6, *"For I am the Lord, I do not change."* Dennis Prager translates this as "I am what I am, I am who I am, I will be what I will be, I will be who I will be.[5]

If God were to change, all His Word would have to change with Him. This would collapse all that God has created, and we would then have no basis for trusting Him.

Since Jesus is the exact representation of God, He never changes. *"Jesus Christ is the same yesterday, today, and forever. Do not be carried about with various and strange doctrines."* (Hebrews 13:8-9) Verse 9 implies that anyone who teaches that God or Jesus has ever or will ever change is teaching a *strange doctrine*. As I've stated in many of my writings, God desires us to know Him so we can know what to expect of Him and so He can be understood. If God did not make Himself known, we could not live by faith. We can only have faith for that of which we are sure!

---

[5] The Rational Bible, Exodus, Dennis Prager, Regnery Faith, Washington DC, 2018, p 44

Many statements and provisions of God are conditional. In other words, certain conditions must be met for us to participate in the benefit. This is not dead works or legalism. The conditions that must be met are generally factors of the heart. The promise has been made, but we must be capable of receiving it in our own hearts! Therefore, the promise is immutable, but the conditions are a matter of our free will.

The first *Law of the Seed* is: *"Every seed yields fruit after its own kind."* (Genesis 1:11) The Hebrew word translated as kind refers to species. While people and plants are able to adapt to weather and other environmental circumstances, the one thing they never do is become another species. Many people ignorantly or deliberately attempt to equate that with Darwinian evolution. But it is not! There is no proof in all the scientific research of one species transforming into another!

This first *Law of the Seed* quite simply means it doesn't matter what we want to happen, how much we pray about it, or what we confess; it doesn't matter what we want to grow in our garden; we will only produce fruit based on the type of seed we plant. This is not dependent on faith or belief. It is an immutable law.

This is why the Apostle Paul issued such a dire warning:

> *Do not be deceived, God is not mocked; for whatever a man sows, that he will also reap. For he who sows to his flesh will of the flesh reap corruption, but he who sows to the Spirit will of the Spirit reap everlasting life.* (Galatians 6:7-8)

Whenever the Bible says, *"Don't be deceived,"* we should pay close attention to what is said next. Evidently, the subject matter is something about which people tend to deceive themselves. We must never deceive ourselves about the *Immutable Law of the Seed*!

There are entire movements and denominations built around a doctrine that contradicts this statement. Regardless of what the doctrine is called or the group that embraces it, they are basically saying since God loves us so much, we can do anything we want with no consequences. This implies that with the New Covenant and the blood of Jesus, God changed. He lowered His standards of ethics and morality.

The Immutable Law of the Seed

These people are far more religious than they think. They incorrectly believe they are enlightened, but their light is darkness (Matthew 6:23). Like most religious people, they surmise that consequences are the product of action taken by God! But the *Law of the Seed* is a law that always operates without God taking any action. The consequence of our beliefs and behavior is the fruit that grows in our lives because of the seeds we have planted.

One of the most insidious lies that has ever been used to turn the world against God is this: God is in control! People incorrectly define sovereignty to mean one of two things: God can do anything He wants to do, or God is in control of everything. If you disagree, they accuse you of not believing God is sovereign.

They fail to grasp that the fruit grows because of the seed that was planted. Consider this: when you plant a garden with tomato seeds, you don't have to pray, and God doesn't have to take action for your garden to produce tomatoes. Likewise, you can't plant tomato seeds and use your faith to get those seeds to produce potatoes. This is the *Law of the Seed*. The law is absolute and unchangeable. But most significant is this: it works without prayer or faith. We can even disbelieve it, and it still works.

Grasping the *Immutable Law of the Seed* takes us through a new portal. In the Hebrew language, the letter "Dalet" is a door, portal, or window that takes us to a new path. Recognizing this path and discovering its secrets doesn't just end a life of continual failure and negative consequences. This opens the door to another dimension of faith beyond what most of us have ever experienced. We can see greater possibilities of life at its best with much less burden on our shoulders.

Remember, when our faith is in the God of creation, we realize that everything God created is an expression of His character. To trust this immutable law is to trust the immutable God who created the law.

Now that you know the *Immutable Law of the Seed*, you pass through the portal when you acknowledge it. In fact, the first step to adopting a new belief is to repent of the old belief you are replacing. Before moving ahead, this would be a great time to accept God's forgiveness for all the times you blamed the consequences of your actions on God!

Divine Prescriptions

- Take time to ponder what God spoke to you in this chapter.
- Ask Him, "In light of what I'm seeing, what are you speaking to me?"
- Then, "How do I apply what I'm seeing to my life?"
- Regardless of How I personally feel about what you're showing me, "You are my Lord. I am willing to follow your leadership."
- I am willing for you to bring me to the place of trusting and applying everything you speak to me."

6. Worn Down By The World

Every day, we are subconsciously being programmed to embrace the World's system and reject God!

Every day, we plant seeds in the garden of our hearts! It can be through conversations, reflecting on something, remembering an event that happened in the past, imagining something that has not actually happened, or complaining about a problem. Whether an internal reflection or external conversation, anytime there is an exchange of information, there is a possibility that we will unknowingly plant it in our heart, and it will begin producing fruit!

Most of what we plant in our hearts happens unintentionally. Our failure to heed Jesus' warning and apply His teachings about the seed renders us oblivious to the wisdom of His teaching. But even when we don't intend for it to happen, seed can be sown that can grow into a crop that forever changes the course of our lives, and it takes no conscious effort on our part.

When the seed we have planted begins to grow, it occurs incrementally. At each stage, the symptoms of that belief grow more powerful until it consumes our lives. We see this in Mark 4:28. Jesus explains the incremental growth of the seed that starts out as information/seed, and then the blade, which could symbolize information, turns into beliefs. Finally, the fruit, which manifests in behavior! Jesus explains, *"For the earth yields crops by itself: first the blade, then the head, after that the full grain in the head."* This parable describes the great majority of believers. They have no awareness of the need, or the know-how to guard their hearts and be careful about what they hear and think. The corrupt information that we take in every day grows, and we don't realize it or understand the process.

We must keep in mind that most of our beliefs are developed unconsciously. Then, one day, we realize our heart is filled with thorns that move our lives onto a destructive path while choking out the good seed we have previously sown. Since we have no idea how it happened, most are oblivious to how it can be corrected! Until we understand how this happens, we are powerless to reverse the syndrome!

> **USUALLY, WHEN OUR BELIEFS BEGIN TO MATERIALIZE INTO WORDS, DEEDS, BEHAVIOR, AND HABITS, WE HAVE NO CLUE WHERE THEY CAME FROM OR WHY WE ARE DOING WHAT WE'RE DOING.**

Usually, when our beliefs begin to materialize into words, deeds, behavior, and habits, we have no clue where they came from or why we are doing what we're doing. All these things come from our hearts because of the seeds we have planted! We usually ignore or justify the emerging signs and symptoms until the problem is taking over parts of our lives. This is all the product of the beliefs of our hearts that were developed because we refused to guard our hearts!

When I do something that is unacceptable, I do it because of a belief. I have that belief because of what I have been exposed to. Conversation then evolves into contemplation, where I nourish those things and cause them to grow. Based on Jesus' teaching about the seed, this is an incredibly simple equation, which means the solution is also simple.

For most of us, there is a tendency to ignore or justify unacceptable behavior. Some people even think it is "legalism" to deal with behavior. I agree that focusing on behavior apart from dealing with beliefs usually ends in some carnal attempt to "do right." But, if we want to walk in love, we have to deal with behavior. Behavior is the outward expression of the heart! Behavior is how we treat others. Beliefs are why we treat others the way we do! Failure to walk in love is expressed through behavior.

But we must always remember that behavior is usually no more than beliefs put into action! To attempt to change the behavior without dealing first with the belief that's driving it never ends well. There should be a commitment to new behavior, but we must never think that changing behavior without changing beliefs is victory. This form of "victory" is actually a work of the flesh, dependent on willpower. The Apostle Paul called this type of ascetic behavior "will worship" and warned that it strengthens the flesh (Colossians 2:23).

Relying on the grace of God is the polar opposite of relying on willpower. Willpower glorifies you; grace glorifies God. The grace of God is an incredibly inclusive truth. It does convey the idea of graciousness and kindness, but functionally, grace is a power, ability, and capacity that works from our heart and comes by unmerited favor.[6] As we persuade our hearts of the truth (righteousness), we are empowered by grace to live that truth/righteousness (Romans 5:1-2).

By dealing with the beliefs of our hearts, we experience a power that is not our own. The "old-timers" called it "the power of the Holy Ghost!" The Baptists call it the fruit of the Spirit. Some groups call it renewal. It doesn't matter if we all share the same terminology; we are all talking about the power of God working in our hearts, making us able to be and do what we cannot be and do in our own strength! When we change our beliefs, our behavior will change… effortlessly!

When teaching about the Kingdom of Heaven and the heart, Jesus warned us while giving us practical instruction about guarding our hearts. *"Be careful what you are hearing."* Why should we be careful? **Everything we hear has the potential to influence our beliefs!** The writer of Proverbs tells us that it is essential that we guard our hearts because our hearts are the source of all that flows in and out of our lives. In fact, our every limiting boundary proceeds from our hearts (Proverbs 4:23).

---

6   (from Thayer's Greek Lexicon, PC Study Bible formatted Electronic Database. Copyright © 2006 by Biblesoft, Inc. All rights reserved.)

Then He explained why this is so important.

> *And He said to them, "Be careful what you are hearing. The measure [of thought and study] you give [to the truth you hear] will be the measure [of virtue and knowledge] that comes back to you — and more [besides] will be given to you who hear."* (Mark 4:24, AMP)

Simply hearing a statement does not mean it goes into our hearts. However, entertaining it, reflecting on it, thinking about it, or talking about it is how it gets planted in our hearts. Paul teaches us how to guard our hearts, which we will discuss in another chapter, but for now, we need to understand that anything we hear, see, or experience, whether it is true or false, has the potential to influence our hearts and thereby affect our lives.

The more we think on, ponder, consider, reflect, talk about, complain about, imagine, or meditate on it, the sooner it takes root in the soil of our hearts, then it begins to grow and ultimately bear fruit. Any information that you talk about, grumble about, think about, gossip about, or worry about until it affects your emotions is a form of biblical meditation. This is how things get written on our hearts. This is how the seeds that have been planted in our hearts grow and produce fruit, i.e., behavior.

Adam and Eve didn't destroy their lives because they believed the serpent; it all started because they were willing to listen to him. Exposure to the ultimate liar was a failure to guard their hearts! We have to guard ourselves from what we see and hear lest we become obsessed and unintentionally begin to meditate on it … Learn the lesson from Lot.

> *God…delivered righteous Lot, who was oppressed*[7] *by the filthy conduct of the wicked (for that righteous man, dwelling among them, tormented his righteous soul from day to day by seeing and hearing their lawless deeds).* (2 Peter 2:7-8)

The word translated as "oppressed" could have been translated as "worn down." We live in a world that is designed to constantly appeal to the lusts of our flesh! The majority of our beliefs were not consciously cho-

---

7 The word oppressed is translated as vexed in the KJV. Strong's translates it as being worn down Biblesoft's New Exhaustive Strong's Numbers and Concordance with Expanded Greek-Hebrew Dictionary. Copyright © 1994, 2003, 2006, 2010 Biblesoft, Inc. and International Bible Translators, Inc.)

sen; they were the result of our constant bombardment of twisted information. Like righteous Lot, even though we are the righteousness of God in Christ, when we continually hear and see the wickedness in the world, we can get worn down!

In Exodus 34:6-7, God reveals one of the many reasons He is able and willing to be so patient and merciful. Moses wanted to see God's glory. God showed him this incredible greatness and splendor by revealing His goodness. *"And the LORD passed by before him, and proclaimed, The LORD, The LORD God, merciful and gracious, longsuffering, and abundant in goodness and truth,"*

The next verse seems to contradict the former. It is usually mistranslated, giving rise to a completely unscriptural doctrine called "generational curses." In The Rational Bible Exodus,[8] Dennis Prager points out that the word translated as "visiting" should be rendered "remembering."

> *Keeping mercy for thousands, forgiving iniquity and transgression and sin, by no means clearing the guilty, visiting **(remembering)** the iniquity of the fathers upon the children and the children's children to the third and the fourth generation.*

God is saying that He will remember that our rebellion and lawlessness were passed down through our families and those who influenced us. We didn't wake up one morning and suddenly decide, "Today, I will rebel against God and destroy my entire life." It was environmental conditioning. We developed most of our faulty beliefs through years of conditioning and repetition by the people in our lives.

When we decide to become disciples of the Lord Jesus, we must become very deliberate about life. We chose the beliefs we now have. Whether by choice or default doesn't matter! But if we intend to participate in the quality of life Jesus is offering, we must choose to "put on" new Biblically-based beliefs.

As you continue in this book, you will discover how to eliminate the destructive seeds you have sown in your heart and replace them with the Word of the Kingdom.

---

[8] The Rational Bible Exodus, Regnery Faith, 2018, Dennis Prager, p 467

The Immutable Law of the Seed

Divine Prescriptions

- Take time to ponder what God spoke to you in this chapter.

- Ask Him, "In light of what I'm seeing, what are you speaking to me?"

- Then, "How do I apply what I'm seeing to my life?"

- Regardless of How I personally feel about what you're showing me, "You are my Lord. I am willing to follow your leadership."

- I am willing for you to bring me to the place of trusting and applying everything you speak to me."

7. The God of Yes

If the answer is always yes, and we trust the One making the promise, there's nothing to pray about!

A promise made by a person of character can always be trusted. There is no need for repeated reassurances. Their word is still good! Once the promise is made, when the receiver is ready to collect, the answer is "yes." There are promises and decisions God has made that will forever be yes. There's nothing left to pray about, unless we don't trust Him!

There are things that are so important to God that He determined in advance how they would proceed, completely independent of our faith, desires, or requests.

Ephesians 1:4-5 tells us, *"He chose us in Him before the foundation of the world."* Before the creation of the heavens and Earth, before man was created, before sin entered into the world, before any person ever prayed and asked God to save them, He predetermined that we would have salvation and come into our ultimate destiny in Christ.

God never decided who would become His sons, but He did decide how we would become sons. It would be by believing in and becoming one with Jesus Christ… *"having predestined us to adoption as sons by Jesus Christ to Himself."*

He also decided that because we would be baptized into His body, we would share in His righteousness and be *holy and blameless*.

All these predetermined acts of God were expressions of His character. He is a God of Life and Love who never desires that anyone would be lost or live a life less than Jesus offered. He didn't wait until we were aware of the need. As Jehovah-Jireh, He saw the need before we prayed and asked for help. He made sure the solution was there waiting for us and gave us the freedom of choice.

These expressions of His character were, by implication, promises. When God expresses Himself through His actions, reinforces it through His Word, and then stakes His name on it, it is a promise and guarantee! Psalm 138:1 says, *"You have exalted above all else Your name and Your word, and You have magnified Your word above all Your name!"* (AMP)

The preceding verse says, *"I will worship toward Your holy temple and praise Your name for Your loving-kindness and for Your truth and faithfulness."* (Psalm 138:2 AMP) This verse reveals that the writer of this Psalm didn't ask God to uphold His name and His Word. He did it because He is always faithful to His own character and nature. In so doing, God was not responding to man; his worship was a response.

> MOST OF WHAT WE NEED FROM GOD HAS ALREADY BEEN TAKEN CARE OF.

Most of what we need from God has already been taken care of. Will I respond to it in complete trust, or will I use my "faith" to seek God's reassurance that He is still faithful? The question begs an answer, "If God has said and staked His name on it, why would I need to use my faith to get Him to be faithful?" That's not faith; that's unbelief! Faith responds to what God has done and who He is, not what we do to get Him to respond to us.

God's promises are not based on something He will do. All His promises are based on what He has already said or done! The answer to all He has already said and done is an unequivocal "Yes!" He is the God of "yes."

Since God's promises are sure, we don't use our faith to convince Him; we use our faith to trust what He has said and done. We persuade our hearts of the reality of His truth. To the degree that our beliefs align with what He has done, we enter into oneness with Him and His truth!

The clearest passage in the entire Bible that tells us the phenomenal power we have when making choices is Deuteronomy 30:19-20: *"I call heaven and earth as witnesses today against you, that I have set before you life and death, blessing and cursing; therefore, choose life."*

It is absolutely within our authority/right/responsibility to make decisions that bring us into harmony with God. It is our choices, not God's, that put us on the path of life or destruction.

Religion has robbed us of our right and responsibility to make these kinds of decisions. Our concepts of faith have been sanitized to protect the self-worth of the faithless. Since we don't believe God's account of creation, we don't see how trusting the natural laws God put in place is an act of faith in God.

The message that is openly stated in this passage debunks the idea that God is making all the choices about whether we live in blessings or curses. Even more incredibly, He offers us the life we want, along with the freedom and responsibility to choose for ourselves.

Religion has convinced us that a miraculous occurrence is when God intervenes and does something that violates the natural laws of physics! This cannot be a correct concept. Here's why! Romans 1:20 tells us, *"God's invisible attributes are clearly seen and understood by the things He made."* If this is true, God's violation of these immutable laws would distort our concept of Him, violating His Word about creation!

In light of God's refusal to violate that which manifests His glory, what is a miracle if not a violation of the laws of physics? Miracles do not occur when we violate the laws of nature; miracles occur when we trust the Creator and His Word about creation! Fortunately, the Bible reveals that there are laws of physics that are beyond our current knowledge.

God has made it possible for us to apply these higher laws. It all starts with how He created all things and proceeds to how He created mankind to interact with creation. All of creation is in harmony with Him. Since the universe and all that is in it was established by His faith, it is responsive to our faith. We don't have to know how the higher laws of physics work. All we need to know is that we have access to those laws when we operate in actual biblical faith. Faith is one of the supreme laws of creation!

A common limiting belief about miracles is that Jesus worked miracles because He is the Son of God. Not only would this conflict with the words of Jesus about having authority because He was the Son of man, but it would also contradict Genesis 1:26, telling us God gave authority on Earth to man. This doctrine possibly brings more responsibility to the human race than anything in the Bible.

If we have authority on planet Earth, it is us, not God, who is introducing all the pain and suffering. If we have authority in almost all things, we never have to wait for God to act; we must choose blessings or curses and live with the results. But remember this: in a world driven by the sin principle, when we do not make a deliberate choice to have the blessings, we have, by default, chosen the curses!

One of the great religious answers that few people know how to answer is this, "What is the will of God?" This brings us to the universal excuse for our ignorance and unbelief in what God has promised. "We will pray and ask God to heal or work a miracle." In modeling the role of man on Earth, Jesus never asked God to heal anyone. He used His authority as the Son of man. Likewise, He didn't tell us to pray for God to heal the sick or work miracles. He said for the believer to do that. How? By using our authority, i.e., his right to act on God's promises

For those who are bold enough to even consider the limitless power of God that works through us, there is a tendency to think we should pray to determine if it's God's will to heal or work a miracle. In so doing, we are not expressing faith in Jesus' finished work, the thousands of promises God has made, the meanings of His covenant names, nor the *Immutable Law of the Seed*; we are actually expressing doubt. We are asking Him to do what He has already done on the Cross. We are asking if He is sure He meant His promises.

God has already made His choice concerning us—blessings. 2 Corinthians 1:20 states, *"All the promises of God in Him are Yes, and in Him Amen, to the glory of God through us."* It is always God's will for us to avoid curses and enjoy the blessings. But we have to choose blessings and the path that leads to the blessings! We have to choose the promises. He will never violate our will by forcing us to participate in His goodness and faithfulness. The word choose means, "a choice, which is based on a thorough examination of the situation and not an arbitrary whim."[9] We seldom make a thorough evaluation of the facts. If we did, His Word, His Name, the life of Jesus, the work of the Cross, and the New Covenant would give us all the relevant information we need to make a choice!

The word "whim" is indicative of something that is done without deliberate conscious thought! Therefore, it is either the product of emotions, habits, or the beliefs of the heart, which is subconscious.

Paul points out God's intentions in 2 Corinthians 1:18-19: *"But as God is faithful, our word to you was not Yes and No. For the Son of God, Jesus Christ, who was preached among you by us... was not Yes and No, but in Him was Yes."*

Paul didn't preach a sometimes *"yes"* and sometimes *"no"* message concerning the promises. This truth contradicts some of our deepest-held traditional religious beliefs. We believe God will change His mind for vague, unexplainable reasons.

All of the New Testament is based on The Old Testament Scriptures, the names of God, the ministry of Jesus, and the New Covenant. Based on these, His answer is always yes. Why? Because that's who He is!

> ALL OF THE NEW TESTAMENT IS BASED ON THE OLD TESTAMENT SCRIPTURES, THE NAMES OF GOD, THE MINISTRY OF JESUS, AND THE NEW COVENANT.

We have a type for God as the *"yes"* God, in an ancient king. Melchizedek was an Old Testament type of Jesus. He was both a king and a priest, just as Jesus is today (Hebrews 7:1-2). The writer of Hebrews, inspired by the Holy Spirit, said of Jesus, *"You are a priest forever According to the order of Melchizedek."* (Hebrews 5:6)

---

9   (from The Complete Word Study Dictionary: Old Testament Copyright © 2003 by AMG Publishers. All rights reserved.)

The Immutable Law of the Seed

In Genesis 4:18, the Hebrew word "priest," describing Melchizedek, is "Ko-hen." Kohen is the word ken with the Hey (H) added right in the middle of the word. Ken is Hebrew for Yes. Hey represents the breath of life breathed into a person or situation. Therefore, Kohen means "a priest to reveal the heart of Yes!"[10] Jesus' priesthood reveals that God has a heart of "Yes." This means that as believers who represent Him on Earth, we should always point out that all the promises are "Yes" in this New Covenant. This includes every promise He ever made to anyone. So, we have to ask, "If God has made a promise, based on His name, His Word, the life, ministry, death, burial, and resurrection of Jesus, and the terms of the New Covenant, do we need to ask Him His will, or should we persuade our hearts and trust in His faithfulness?

Divine Prescriptions

- Take time to ponder what God spoke to you in this chapter.

- Ask Him, "In light of what I'm seeing, what are you speaking to me?"

- Then, "How do I apply what I'm seeing to my life?"

- Regardless of How I personally feel about what you're showing me, "You are my Lord. I am willing to follow your leadership."

- I am willing for you to bring me to the place of trusting and applying everything you speak to me."

---

[10] Hebrew Word Pictures, 2020, Frank T Seekins, p. 54

8. The Subconscious Filter

When there is a battle between the conscious mind and the heart, the heart always wins!

I have heard much wonderful teaching about the need to get control of our thoughts. I fully agree with the concept. One's life will never become stable or consistent beyond the ability and willingness to gain control of one's thought life. However, if we don't know how to influence our hearts, we will never get control of our thoughts. Trying to control your thoughts is a tiresome battle that never ends unless we deal with it at a heart level.

It is absolutely essential that we learn how to do *HeartWork*[11] if we want any degree of control over our thoughts. In my book, *Moving Your Invisible Boundaries*,[12] we take a deep dive into the biblical difference between the heart and the mind and how we can utilize that information to bring our heart and mind into harmony with God. This will be a slight review of that material with many significant additions.

The book of Proverbs tells us about the Doorkeeper of the Heart. This is so crucial because a doorkeeper determines what gets in and out of the door. A dishonest doorkeeper will let other criminals into our house if he

---
11   https://heartphysics.com/
12   https://www.truepotentialmedia.com/product/moving-your-invisible-boundaries/

is left guarding the entrance. The Hebrew language presents the concept of an internal door or portal that leads to a new path. That path can lead us to blessings or curses.

Proverbs 23:7 says, *"...as he **thinks** in his heart, so is he."* The word *"think"* in Hebrew means a door, gate, or portal, and a janitor, or keeper, rendering the concept of a doorkeeper.[13] The Hebrew letters that are used to spell *"think"* indicate that a person can be consumed with their thoughts to such a degree that it alters the understanding of their heart and how they perceive things. We must always remember that the things we think about are the seeds we are planting in our hearts.

What does it actually mean to "think with our heart?" The thoughts of the heart are subconscious. All that means is that these thoughts occur below our conscious awareness. The thoughts of the heart are not based on the information you are consciously taking in. They are based on your beliefs about what you are seeing, hearing, or experiencing! To a great degree, the heart actually interprets and adds significance to what we see or hear.

Let's say that sometime in your life, you were attacked by a dog. When we have good or bad experiences, we usually pass judgment about "why it happened." You may judge that this was a violent dog, and you will avoid it in the future. Or, you may judge that all dogs are violent so they are a threat to your safety and should be avoided. If this is your judgment, when you encounter a dog, even a gentle dog, you will feel fearful emotions emerging. Your reaction may become unreasonable. Any time we find ourselves overacting to something that is happening in the present, it is usually based on a negative past experience. Our out-of-character response is caused by the thoughts of the heart, which are the product of our beliefs!

When an irrational experience is over, you may have no understanding of why your emotions and reactions were so extreme. It's simple! The doorkeeper of your heart opened the door for your fear of dogs to be fully experienced and expressed. Your beliefs about dogs stimulate the thoughts of your heart. But none of this was conscious.

---

13 (Biblesoft's New Exhaustive Strong's Numbers and Concordance with Expanded Greek-Hebrew Dictionary. Copyright © 1994, 2003, 2006, 2010 Biblesoft, Inc. and International Bible Translators, Inc.)

So, we see that the seed that was deposited in our hearts from our judgment about the initial negative experience with dogs is bringing forth fruit after its kind. When we plant the seeds of fear, it always produces more fear. When we plant the seeds of peace, we have more peace. It is an immutable law; we reap what we sow, and every seed bears after its kind!

The heart tends to communicate via subconscious thoughts that seem more like intuition or even impulses than thoughts. Your conscious mind can be constantly saying, "I will not be afraid; I will not be afraid," all while you are yielding to the irrational emotions of fear. How does this happen? The doorkeeper releases the fruit of the seed that was planted in your heart! And the heart always wins over the intentions of the mind. One source says the power and influence of the heart is 5000 times more powerful than the thoughts of the mind!

> THE HEART TENDS TO COMMUNICATE VIA SUBCONSCIOUS THOUGHTS THAT SEEM MORE LIKE INTUITION OR EVEN IMPULSES THAN THOUGHTS.

Just like the doorkeeper allows the beliefs of your heart to direct your conscious mind, allowing undesirable things to come out, it can also allow undesirable things to enter. These beliefs of the heart are why so many people hear the Word of the Kingdom but never understand it.

Remember Lot, we discussed in a previous chapter, was a righteous man. He was not involved in the sins of Sodom and Gomorrah. But he did not guard his heart; he remained in that wicked environment. Just the fact that he saw and heard their wicked deeds wore him down. Had the Lord not delivered him, he would have no doubt succumbed to the pressure and temptation.

As a pastor and counselor, I have witnessed that most people who became abusers were people who had been abused. Or, those who witnessed atrocities often committed those same crimes, even though the mere thought of what they experienced is repulsive. You would think, due to their painful experiences, they would be the most compassionate and least likely to commit the same acts against others that were perpetrated against them. None of it seems logical until you understand the *Immutable Law of the Seed*.

The Immutable Law of the Seed

There is a Scriptural concept that I explain like this. You become what you behold! Hearing and seeing are seeds that we can either discard or hold. But holding them, even in contempt, facilitates the seed being planted in our hearts.

Wherever you place your attention, even if you find it disgusting, it will eventually wear you down, vexing your soul. When it does, you will find yourself drawn to it… unless you know how to deal with it in your heart! For the believer, this is a matter of sending away, i.e., putting off the old man, renewing the mind, and putting on the new man. Renewing the mind is all about planting the seed of God's Word about your identity in Christ, what you have in Him, and what you can do through Him!

Things go on around us that we can't escape them as long as we are in this world. We may not participate or find it appealing, but it can eventually become a seed planted in our hearts. Since, however, we understand the *Law of the Seed*, we can avoid all the religious antics of screaming at the devil, torturing and condemning ourselves, which only plants more seeds that will continue to choke out the Word of the Kingdom!

Jesus provided a great analogy to understand the problem and the cure. We are like people who bathed and then walked for several miles in sandals. Even though our bodies are clean, our feet have become soiled by walking through this world. In this example, Jesus revealed something that is easy to overlook.

> *Jesus… rose from supper and laid aside His garments, took a towel, and girded Himself. After that, He poured water into a basin and began to wash the disciples' feet, and to wipe them with the towel with which He was girded. Then He came to Simon Peter. And Peter said to Him, "Lord, are You washing my feet?" 7 Jesus answered and said to him, "What I am doing you do not understand now, but you will know after this." Peter said to Him, "You shall never wash my feet!" Jesus answered him,* **"If I do not wash you, you have no part with Me."** *Simon Peter said to Him, "Lord, not my feet only, but also my hands and my head!" Jesus said to him, "He who is bathed needs only to wash his feet; but is completely clean.* (John 13:4-10)

Even though we have been washed in the blood of Jesus, we can have experiences that affect our hearts. We don't need to be "saved" again, but we do need to deal with how we have been affected. Several passages in the New Testament refer to the cleansing of the conscience for believers.

The conscience is the voice of the heart. The word conscience is a compound word that means "dual knowledge." It is the voice of our spirit where God continually testifies that we are the righteousness of God in Christ, and then there is the voice of the soul that testifies to our deeds. When these two are not in harmony, our conscience is violated. In our inner man, we feel disharmony. This is when we need our "feet washed." This is obviously metaphoric for allowing ourselves to continually be cleansed and renewed. This recovery begins with a personal connection to Jesus and His work on the Cross. Then, we renew our minds by planting new seeds in the garden of our hearts. These seeds take us into the final phase of this process. They begin to bear fruit in the likeness of Jesus (Ephesians 4:20-24).

1 John 1:9 has been misapplied by many different groups. Although its goal is to bring us back into harmony with God, many use it to condemn. It seems that most turn it into a religious ritual that has no positive effect on our hearts.

This is not saying, "You have become unrighteous because of your failures." But it is saying that unrighteous behavior or exposure is bringing some degree of darkness into your life. The goal of dealing with this issue is to return to a place where your heart does not condemn you. When condemnation is gone, one can emerge from the darkness and return to a place of harmony and fellowship with Him. This is what it means for us to allow Jesus to wash our feet.

He said that if we don't allow Him to wash our feet when needed, we have no "part with Him." The Greek for "part" refers to a share or allotment. This does not imply we have lost our salvation, but it clearly communicates the fact that we need to return to the place in our hearts where we share in His resurrected life and inheritance. When our heart condemns us, we lose confidence before God, and faith becomes difficult. That's why the Apostle John said it could bring us to the place where we can't receive answers to our prayers (1 John 3:20-22). It is not saying that God does not hear and respond. The inability to have answered prayer is determined by the condition of our hearts, not a change in God's heart toward us.

The alienation we feel when we walk in selfishness or other sins is not God rejecting us; it is our heart condemning us. The alienation is in our minds. Many times, we don't know why we feel distant from God. Very often, it is just the effects of living and walking through a wicked world. One should never waste time trying to figure out what they did wrong. Like the Old Testament worshipers, we simply need to *"… draw near with a true heart in full assurance of faith, having our hearts sprinkled from an evil conscience."* (Hebrews 10:22)

It is in these times that we remind ourselves that we are washed in His blood. Jesus has forgiven all our sins and trespasses. Remind yourself of everything that is yours in Jesus. Glorify God by acknowledging your new identity with Him. These are seeds that will not only produce fruit after their own kind, but they will choke out the thorns we have sown in our hearts!

> **THE MORE WE PLANT THE SEEDS OF OUR IDENTITY IN CHRIST, THE MORE FRUIT WE WILL PRODUCE, AFFECTING OUR THOUGHTS AND OUR BEHAVIOR.**

The more we plant the seeds of our identity in Christ, the more fruit we will produce, affecting our thoughts and our behavior. We will create a new doorkeeper. It will become natural for us to filter out those thoughts and impulses that would lead us into unrighteous, i.e., self-destructive behavior. We determine what will be the doorkeeper of our hearts by the seeds we plant

Then, we need to follow the advice of the Scripture and separate ourselves from the environmental influences that negatively affect us, whether in a conscious or subconscious way, Proverbs 1:15. The more we hear, see, and think about the ungodly things around us, the more seed we plant that will choke out the Word of the Kingdom.

Everything we hear, see, and experience is a seed that can be planted in our hearts. Choose wisely and avoid that which leads to temptation, condemnation, and darkness!

Divine Prescriptions

- Take time to ponder what God spoke to you in this chapter.

- Ask Him, "In light of what I'm seeing, what are you speaking to me?"

- Then, "How do I apply what I'm seeing to my life?"

- Regardless of How I personally feel about what you're showing me, "You are my Lord. I am willing to follow your leadership."

- I am willing for you to bring me to the place of trusting and applying everything you speak to me."

9. Habits or Choices

When something becomes real in our hearts, it requires no conscious effort!

So many of the repetitive conflicts that occur between married couples, friends, or in the workplace are seldom the result of conscious decisions. Usually, these conflicts, especially those involving emotional outbursts, are nothing more than habits. They are not the results of weighing the outcome, considering how they will affect the relationship or what they will cost us in stress, conflict, or money.

So we must ask, how do we develop habits? Habits are automatic, subconscious actions we have programmed into our minds. They can be created by doing the same thing over and over. Eventually, our nervous system, along with muscle memory, is programmed to follow a pattern of thoughts and behaviors in response to certain stimuli.

In certain cases involving extreme reactions or irrational thinking, this is more than muscle memory. This is the result of consciously or subconsciously establishing beliefs that have become something we do without giving them a conscious thought.

God created us with the ability to develop habits. Habits, since they are part of our natural make-up, are not inherently good or evil. However, we can use them for good or evil. Any ability or capacity given to us at creation was given for our good but can be used for evil, by choice or habit. We know natural capabilities are good because, after each day of Creation, God assessed His work and said, *"It is good!"* This includes the creation of the human race!

As previously discussed, the Hebrew word that is translated as "good' means more than pleasant, desirable, well-pleasing, and morally correct. According to Chaim Bentorah, in his book, *Learning God's Love Language*,[14] the word "good" is always a reference to "harmony." In other words, what made all of creation good was the fact that it was in harmony with God's character and nature, but it was also in harmony with His goals and intentions.

When God created man, we have a greater understanding of the harmony He sought. Before sin was introduced, Earth was in perfect harmony with God. This means that to be compatible with God's creation; man also had to be created in the perfect likeness and image of God so Earth and man would be in perfect harmony, just as God and Earth were in harmony.

On the sixth day, the last thing God created was man. I can only assume, based on the sequence, as described in Scripture, that God created man just before the beginning of the Sabbath. This meant that his first day on Earth was a day of rest, designed specifically so he would begin his life in communion with God! This is a model for us, one in which all our endeavors should begin with ensuring our intentions are in harmony with our Creator. He cannot be an afterthought.

One of the most important subtle nuances between the sixth day of creation and all the previous days is the fact that on the day that He created man, He didn't say it was good. He declared that it was **very good!** *"Then God saw everything that He had made, and indeed it was **very good**. So the evening and the morning were the sixth day."* (Genesis 1:31)

In English, God said, now that man is created, all of creation is abundantly good. None of creation could reach the pinnacle of purpose until it was inhabited by man, who was to be the representative of God on Earth.

---

14   https://www.truepotentialmedia.com/product/learning-gods-love-language-book-workbook-bundle/

Adam and all of creation were flawless. None of God's creation was evil. There was no sin, sickness, death, or lack of any kind. Many groups have ignorantly assigned evil to different animals, inherent capabilities of humans, and even some of the laws of physics. But God said it was all "very good!" Nothing in God's creation is inherently evil! But all things can be used for evil.

Even though we no longer have a sinful nature, we still have memories of how we functioned in the world's system. When we don't trust that God is a good God and He will give us a way to fulfill our desires that will not destroy us, we turn to the world's system to fulfill our desires.

> **EVEN THOUGH WE NO LONGER HAVE A SINFUL NATURE, WE STILL HAVE MEMORIES OF HOW WE FUNCTIONED IN THE WORLD'S SYSTEM.**

According to some research, our long-term memories are stored in our hearts. Our lifetime of memories becomes the basis for our identity. Thus, this is the source of our sense of identity before we come to Christ. Those memories are now dormant and will remain so unless we feed them. If we continue to think about ourselves as we were in the past and fail to renew our minds in Christ, we will repopulate our hearts with seeds about our past that recreate the past. They will grow and produce fruit, i.e., beliefs and behaviors that are no different than how we lived before we came to Christ. But this is all based on memories, not sinful nature!

These memories, stored in the heart, are not necessarily conscious memories. They are mostly subconscious. A subconscious memory is like a computer program. No matter what you type, based on conscious thought, the program still defines certain limitations, boundaries, and capabilities of the computer. Since we are typing and seeing our work on the screen, we incorrectly think we are in control. That's much the way it is with our lives. We think our conscious mind is in control. But it isn't!

Our conscious thought does have limited, momentary control within parameters defined by our beliefs. But we cannot permanently supersede the programming of the heart unless we plant new seeds in our hearts concerning our new identity! Remember, when there is a conflict between the mind and the heart, the heart always wins. The failure to establish new beliefs is the reason the believer keeps cycling through the same failures and issues.

Throughout our lives, we have developed hundreds of habits. Some research indicates that between 45% and 95% of our behaviors are the product of habits. This means that half or more of everything we do is not done deliberately; it is not done by intelligently choosing an outcome we desire. As the old saying goes, it's functioning like a person ready to fire a gun without aiming. "Ready, fire, aim!" There's no telling what or who will be hurt by the lack of present-tense deliberate choices!

This is why repentance is so powerful. Repentance, which includes renewing the mind, is designed to help us after we have acted irresponsibly. However, renewing the mind, which includes repentance, can be done before the damage is inflicted. It is the fruit of a person who has planted seeds of righteousness, peace, and joy in their hearts. They have pre-programmed themselves. They have a filter that will check their impulses before action is taken!

Many of our habits are developed subconsciously. When we are exposed to something over and over, like when we see how our parents and other influential people respond to certain stimuli, or even when watching television and hundreds of other arenas of input, we are gathering information. What we see, hear, and experience will eventually "vex" us just as the inhabitants of Sodom and Gomorrah vexed *righteous Lot*. If we think on these things, we eventually will eventually mimic those behaviors, or we will be repulsed by them and flee from them. But be assured, when we are repeatedly exposed to anything, an internal choice will eventually be made! With no conscious thought, we often choose a path with no consideration of where that path will lead us.

Upon becoming a new creation in Christ, our first responsibility is to realize the old man is dead, discover who we are "in Christ," what we have "in Christ," and what we can do "in Christ." This should begin at water baptism. We have been given a new identity that will never reach its fullest potential if it is not developed in both our hearts and minds! This happens by renewing the mind and putting on the new man!

When we were born again, God gave us a new heart. But we still have free will. How we develop our hearts from that point is up to us.

If we were actually discipled, we would immediately learn the three aspects of the gospel: what happened on the Cross, what happened in the grave, and what happened through the resurrection.

We would be taught the biblical concept of transformation, which occurs when we become one with Christ in each of those phases of the gospel. This is called reconciliation, i.e., exchange.

We all go through a renewal process after we get a new heart. We either plant seeds of righteousness that grow and bear the fruit of righteousness, or we plant the seeds of memories, allowing our past struggles, fears, and limitations to grow in our hearts. These deep-seated memories create habits that drive our choices, with no conscious awareness of the decisions we are making.

Divine Prescriptions

In the Hebrew language, the instructions, corrections, and warnings in God's Word are considered Divine Prescriptions. Prescriptions tend to both prevent illness and cure it.

- Take time to ponder what God spoke to you in this chapter.
- Ask Him, "In light of what I'm seeing, what are you speaking to me?"
- Then, "How do I apply what I'm seeing to my life?"
- Regardless of How I personally feel about what you're showing me, "You are my Lord. I am willing to follow your leadership."
- I am willing for you to bring me to the place of trusting and applying everything you speak to me."

Section II: The Sower and The Seed

10. The Sower

Everyone who communicates anything is a Sower. What they communicate is the seed!

A Sower is merely someone who scatters seeds (words/information). Seeds are words. As such, all words have the potential to be planted in our hearts and affect the way we think and believe.

It is our responsibility to guard our hearts against words and thoughts that grow into destructive beliefs but open our hearts to the Word of God. One of the most effective ways to guard our hearts is to use wisdom about what and to whom we expose ourselves.

In addition to what we hear, we must guard what we allow ourselves to see. Seeing is not actually speaking words until we turn them into words in our thoughts. When we look at Lot's life, we get some concept of how dramatically seeing and hearing can influence our character.

We know that Lot was a righteous man, but he was worn down and oppressed by *seeing and hearing* the wickedness of the people of Sodom (2 Peter 2:7).

We don't know the specifics about how his environment influenced him, but we do know that the angel had to forcibly deliver him from this wicked city that was about to be destroyed (Genesis 19:16). It seems that he had lost spiritual sensitivity to such a degree that he felt comfortable in Sodom's wickedness. We also know that his wife longingly looked back at Sodom and was destroyed (Genesis 19:26).

The Scripture provides an abundance of warnings concerning the words we speak, the words we hear, and our own inner dialog.

God's word warns us to set a watch over our mouths to guard what we say and to guard our hearts in what we hear, see, and think.

> THE SOWER CAN BE ANYONE, INCLUDING OURSELVES.

The Sower can be anyone, including ourselves. The Sower scatters seeds intentionally or unintentionally. Regardless of his or her intention, they can be seeds of life or death. But make no mistake: All words are seeds, and all words, including our internal dialog, have the potential to be sown in our hearts to become beliefs that lead us to life or death. *"Death and life are in the power of the tongue."* (Proverbs 18:21)

Proverbs 10:19 says, *"In the multitude of words sin is not lacking, But he who restrains his lips is wise."*

This particular Hebrew word translated as "sin" is very unique. The root is spelled Pei, Shen, and Ayin. Each of these letters has its own definition, which greatly broadens our understanding of the word.

Pei is a reference to the mouth and the power of speech.

Shen refers to destruction, corruption, or total annihilation.

Ayin addresses perception, entering into light or darkness, positive or negative, life or death

The idea conveyed through a combination of these letters and the general translation of this word for sin would be something like this:

Speaking too many careless words can so alter one's perception which could potentially lead one into darkness and even total annihilation.

While this verse more specifically refers to spoken words, based on an abundance of other Scriptures, we can deduce that thinking and pondering on the words we hear is how they are sown in our hearts.

Proverbs 12:6 explains it like this, *"The words of the wicked are, "Lie in wait for blood," But the mouth of the upright will deliver them."*

The phrase "lie in wait" means to lurk, and wait to ambush.[15] In future chapters, we will discuss in detail, the fact that the words can "go get inside of us."

The words of the wicked are corrupt; they can plunge us into chaos, darkness, and disorder. This doesn't happen just because we hear those words spoken. It's what we do with them internally that determines the degree to which they can affect us.

If we hold to those words and reflect on them, they can take hold in our minds, then our hearts, and at the opportune time they will ambush us to "take our blood."

One way we guard our hearts is by being selective about the people with whom we surround ourselves.

Numerous Scriptures warn us to use wisdom and discretion concerning the type of people with whom we spend time. The NIV says, *"Do not be misled: 'Bad company corrupts good character.'"* (1 Corinthians 15:33)

While we have no intention of learning their ways, it still happens. Sometimes, it happens because we begin to desire their way of life, but sometimes it is because we despise their way of life.

Wherever we place our attention, whether it is something we desire or something we despise, it has the power to vex us. Just the fact that it gets our attention and creates emotions means it is a seed that is being planted in the garden of our hearts.

The most important thing over which we have stewardship is our own heart. We must constantly guard our hearts from the pernicious seeds that we unwittingly planted in our hearts simply by what we see and hear!

I often say, "Adam's failure, in the garden didn't begin because he believed the lies of the serpent. No! The problem began when he was willing to have a conversation with a known liar. By exposing himself to a liar, the

---

15   (from The Complete Word Study Dictionary: Old Testament Copyright © 2003 by AMG Publishers. All rights reserved.)

seeds of destruction were planted in his heart. In other words, he didn't guard his heart! So, we must ask ourselves, what am I exposing myself to, and what potential effect could it have on my heart?

Despite this valuable Life Lesson we learn from Adam and the serpent, we haphazardly engage in conversations with liars, gossips, slanders, discord sowers, and those who undermine our confidence, as if they do not affect us.

If we have any intention of taking God's warnings seriously, we must guard our hearts from exposure to that which could corrupt us. We deceive ourselves into thinking that there's a line that we will not cross. If we see someone influencing us in a destructive manner, we believe we are committed to putting distance between ourselves and that person.

That plan seldom works. As we expose ourselves to certain ways of thinking, we soon stop being shocked at what we're hearing because we are slowly being conditioned.

Once we are conditioned, we no longer block out the words and behavior that were once so shocking. The following verse is applicable to any destructive behavior. *"Make no friendship with an angry man, And with a furious man do not go, Lest you **learn** his ways And set a snare for your soul."* (Proverbs 22:24-25)

The Hebrew phrase means to learn by association. It is not intentional learning. It is learning by association, repetition, and subconscious influence.

We can easily become like those whom we never intended to copy by repetitive exposure. Like Adam in the garden with the serpent. Our failure is not that we believe and yield to corrupt people. Our failure is that we keep exposing ourselves to them.

The upside of Proverbs 12:6 is this: just as we can be influenced by words or darkness, death, and destruction, we can recover by speaking, pondering, reflecting, and meditating on the Word of life. *"But the mouth of the upright will deliver them."* (Proverbs 12:6)

There is the upright mouth that speaks words of righteousness, and there is the mouth of the wicked, which spews words that lead to death. Therefore, guarding our hearts is not merely avoiding bad conversations; it is surrounding ourselves with those who fully love and trust God.

Everyone is a Sower, and everyone is a seed planter, whether they intend to or not! Regardless, however, to whom we expose ourselves, we have the final determination of how the words we hear will affect us. We give the words we hear the power of life and death by the degree we think about them or repetitively hear them!

In a subsequent chapter, we will discuss the continuum of how words morph into thoughts, beliefs, and, ultimately, a way of life!

Divine Prescription

In the Hebrew language, the instructions, corrections, and warnings in God's Word are considered Divine Prescriptions. Prescriptions tend to both prevent illness and cure it.

- Take time to ponder what God spoke to you in this chapter.
- Ask Him, "In light of what I'm seeing, what are you speaking to me?"
- Then, "How do I apply what I'm seeing to my life?"
- Regardless of How I personally feel about what you're showing me, "You are my Lord. I am willing to follow your leadership."
- I am willing for you to bring me to the place of trusting and applying everything you speak to me."

11. The Propagation of The Seed

Propagation of both good and evil is always the work of disciples!

Jesus presented another parable about the Kingdom of Heaven, commonly known as the Parable of the Wheat and Tares. In this parable, the seeds of both the wheat and the tares represent people who sow either good or bad seeds.

In this parable, He reveals the mystery of how both good and evil are propagated and how they have multiplied through the generations. Well-intentioned but misguided people have misunderstood the propagation of good and evil. In grasping for answers that seem logical, they make the devil appear to be nearly as powerful as God. They unintentionally imply that the devil is omnipresent, i.e., he can be everywhere at once, whispering in the ears of millions of people. This religious error causes us to misunderstand how evil is propagated, thereby reducing our effectiveness at thwarting Satan's plans. Unlocking this mystery Will not only give us great insight into how we must guard our hearts but also how to influence the world around us for the Kingdom!

I would recommend that before progressing in this chapter, you read the parable of the wheat and tares, as well as its explanation (Matthew

13:24-30 and 36-43). Keep in mind that this parable provides greater insight into the parable of the Sower and the Seed. It is an expansion of the *Immutable Law of the Seed*! What starts as the seed going into and influencing a believer escalates into a lifestyle that influences others.

Keep in mind that a student wants to know what his master knows, but a disciple desires to live like their master. Both the godless and the godly are disciples of their master's lifestyle, even when they don't realize who their master is!

Christians think that winning the world happens by merely preaching the Word to sinners. Satanists and other occult groups don't reach the world by the message they preach as much as by the lifestyle they live. They realize that influence is more powerful than information alone!

Sinners aren't going into the world attempting to convert others to share in their beliefs. They invite others to join the party, have fun, and gratify their desires. In fact, true Satanists, cults, and secret societies don't want you to know what they believe until you are addicted to their lifestyle. This is part of the secret to their effectiveness at propagating their evil message. They first want you to become a disciple, i.e., live as they live. This eventually opens one's heart to their corrupt message.

The church has endeavored to make converts and students instead of disciples, as the Lord Jesus mandated, Matthew 28:19-20. It seems that believers think the world will be won with information alone. Consequently, they have created generations of students attempting to live as "Christians" through intellectual information instead of disciples living by the power of God's grace.

Jesus taught the Word of God, but His true "superpower" for influence was how He lived. He was the Word in the flesh. The observers witnessed a quality of life-based on God's Word that had never been seen or considered. They were deeply influenced by the fact that He had authority. His words were powerful, but what drew people to Him was the way He lived (Matthew 7:28-29).

Biblical discipleship to the Lord Jesus is almost nonexistent in the 21st-century church. People become disciples of a leader who impresses them; they become disciples of a particular group or message, but our lives don't necessarily represent the values of God. Therefore, our message and our lives are out of sync, making the world doubt and sometimes despise the believer and never seek the truth about God!

Jesus never told us to make converts; He told us to make disciples. As such, we should teach them to *"observe all things that I (Jesus) have commanded you."* (Matthew 28:20) In tandem with the message we preach, we must model what that message looks like. More than any other area, we must reflect our faith in the way we treat them. We should treat them just as Jesus would treat them, and we should treat one another as Jesus treated His disciples. Teaching that is not backed up by modeling comes across as hypocritical. Therefore, the way we treat one another is equally influential. *"Jesus said it like this, 'By this all will know that you are My disciples, if you have love for one another.'"* (John 13:35)

> JESUS NEVER TOLD US TO MAKE CONVERTS; HE TOLD US TO MAKE DISCIPLES.

If we follow Jesus' model of teaching, we combine sharing the Word to reveal God's true intentions, modeling that Word to see what it looks like in application, allowing them to ask questions, and then showing them how to put it into practice, and following up by answering more questions. He didn't merely teach line upon line; He modeled the lifestyle and benefits of living the Word, allowing them to observe and ask questions!

Disciples are the propagators of their masters. According to this parable, the good seed represents the sons of the Kingdom, and the tares are the sons of the wicked one. The field represents the world (Matthew 13:38-39).

It is not the devil who whispers in people's ears, nor is it Jesus who always personally speaks to every individual. It is the disciples who propagate and multiply not just their message but their lifestyles to the world. We are the voice of God or the voice of the evil one proclaiming our master's message while making disciples of our lifestyle!

Please understand I'm not saying that Jesus, through the Holy Spirit, does not speak into people's hearts. I am saying that people who are not born again cannot perceive the Kingdom; they can't fathom surrendering their lives to Jesus as Lord. Consequently, they are not willing to hear, understand, and obey. Jesus commissioned us to be the light of the world. What people do recognize is when the Word is working in our lives. They learn by the way we treat them and what they see in our lives.

You may be wondering why this is significant!

The Parable of the Sower is the first phase of the *Immutable Law of the Seed*. This reveals how every seed reproduces after its kind in the soil of our hearts. This is how the seed affects us personally. The Parable of the Wheat and Tares, however, expands the Immutable *Law of the Seed* by depicting how the seed in our hearts produces behavior that sows seeds in the world... as a result of what is in our hearts!

At the end of the day, the church has lost this battle. We ignored Jesus' mandate to make disciples. Instead, in our unscriptural zeal, we became like the world to attract the world. But the more we became like them, the less we had to offer when they came!

It is important that we realize that this parable is not an expanded dichotomy between wheat and thorns. Thorns are easy to identify because they look so different from wheat. However, tares look and sound so much like wheat that the master was concerned that in their attempt to pull up the tares, they would likely pull up the wheat as well. This presents a dichotomy between the wheat and the tares!

The corrupting factor of the tares is their ability to hide in plain sight. They can have every appearance of being true believers, with one exception: the tares never bear fruit. Keep in mind that there are those who are "tares" by choice, but in the church, the tares are people who have every appearance of being believers but never become fruit-bearing disciples. They don't, however, identify as disciples; they identify as Christians. Why? They don't actually know the difference because of the watered-down messages they have heard.

Tares never become disciples of the Lord Jesus. They may live good moral and ethical lives, but their hearts do not yield the fruit of righteousness. They do not produce a consistent life of righteousness. It is not, however, our responsibility to identify and eradicate them. Neither should we soften our message to appease them.

Since tares are not open to the Word of the Kingdom or the Lordship of Jesus, they infiltrate churches and bring a carnal influence. They want leadership based on carnal principles. They want humanistic programs instead of discipleship programs. They measure success by the size of the congregation and its budget! They become the leaven that works its way through an entire congregation, bringing compromise and chaos to everything significant about being a disciple. The world thinks that since they are in church and call themselves Christians, they must be true believers. But their lack of bearing the fruit inflames the unbeliever, driving them into harsh judgment against what looks like a compromised church.

The parable reveals several important factors.

It is not our responsibility to pass judgment and determine who are wheat and who are the tares. We should stick to our mandate to make disciples. Continuing to make disciples will usually separate the Tares from the Wheat without causing conflict in our congregation!

This also fulfills Jesus' teaching that we know people by the fruit they bear, not by the words they speak.

Last and most important is the fact that Jesus Himself will sort out the wheat and the tares in the end! It's not our "ministry!"

Divine Prescriptions

Take time to ponder what God spoke to you in this chapter.

- Ask Him, "In light of what I'm seeing, what are you speaking to me?"
- Then, "How do I apply what I'm seeing to my life?"
- Regardless of How I personally feel about what you're showing me, "You are my Lord. I am willing to follow your leadership."
- I am willing for you to bring me to the place of trusting and applying everything you speak to me."

12. The Wayside

The Devil can only do what we allow Him to do!

We all know we have a great enemy, i.e., *"That serpent of old, called the Devil and Satan, who deceives the whole world."* (Revelation 12:9) He uses deception because he has no authority to attack us. Once we are deceived, we yield to him through fear and unbelief!

We know he is a thief, murderer, and liar. The Bible reveals his character and intentions through multiple names and a myriad of descriptive terms that describe him and his behavior. But we should never forget that he is not more powerful than we are. *"You are of God, little children, and have overcome them, because He who is in you is greater than he who is in the world."* (1 John 4:4)

Sometimes, we miss the obvious about the devil because we tend to think of him as the horned, evil one, dressed in a red suit, with a pointed tail, carrying a pitchfork! Little of what we believe about the devil is actually consistent with Scripture. Secular, occult-based society has inundated us with images of the devil that frighten us. Through these images, we lose sight of his defeat at the resurrection and his limited power, *"Having disarmed principalities and powers, He made a public spectacle of them, triumphing over them in it."* (Colossians 2:15)

Through religion, we have created an evil persona that keeps us from seeing him as he is. The unscriptural caricature we have created in our imagination makes it difficult for us to clearly identify him and easily defeat him! Maybe we should stop embracing any concept of the devil that is not clear in Scripture.[16]

All these things we believe about the devil, when pondered and reflected, become seeds that get planted in our hearts. When we plant seeds of fear, we produce a new crop of fear. This unscriptural thinking, when planted in the soil of our hearts, chokes out the good seed of the Kingdom that would make us bold as lions in the presence of the wicked one!

One of the most corrupt seeds we sow about the devil is an unscriptural idea that man gave his authority to Satan when he yielded to sin. I know, based on circumstances, it seems that way, but that is an illusion.

> **THERE ISN'T ANY SCRIPTURE THAT SAYS WE LOST OUR AUTHORITY TO THE DEVIL.**

There isn't any Scripture that says we lost our authority to the devil. In my book *Satan Unmasked*, we discuss this prophecy in Isaiah 14:12, which has a double fulfillment. One is about a human king, and the other is about a fallen spiritual being, which is asked the question: *"How you are fallen from heaven, O Lucifer, son of the morning!* ***How you are cut down to the ground****, You who weakened the nations!"*

In the "man lost authority" doctrine, we forget three things: 1) There is no Scriptural validation for that doctrine, 2) Satan was never given authority over planet Earth, but mankind was, and 3) all angels were created to be servants to those who would inherit salvation.

If falling into sin and rebellion would strip anyone of authority, Satan would be at the top of that list. He not only went into rebellion, but he also led both the angels and man into rebellion. So, if he had any authority, he would have lost it!

Isaiah 14:16 tells us a day will come when we will see Satan as he really is, and we will be surprised that we gave him so much opportunity to work

---

16 *Satan Unmasked*, reveals the authority we have over the devil and frees us from an unjustified fear.

in our world! *"Those who see you will gaze at you, And consider you, saying: 'Is this the man who made the earth tremble, who shook kingdoms…"*

We can wait until Jesus binds him and throws him into the abyss to finally see him for who and what he really is. Then, we will realize we could have overcome him any time we chose to believe the truth. So, the question remains, "What is the truth about Satan?"

The truth is, whatever glory or power he possessed before his fall, he lost it at the resurrection. We too quickly abandon what Jesus accomplished at the Cross and buy into some pop theology. Here's what Jesus did: *"Having disarmed principalities and powers, He made a public spectacle of them, triumphing over them in it."* (Colossians 2:15)

If Satan is stripped, how has he created such destruction for the human race? The answer is simple: He is an opportunist enemy. In other words, he can only do what we allow him to do.

Temptation doesn't start with the devil; it starts with our desires.

> *But each one is tempted when he is drawn away by his own desires and enticed. Then, when desire has conceived, it gives birth to sin; and sin, when it is full-grown, brings forth death.* (James 1:14-15)

You may notice that in this continuum of sin and death, there is actually no mention of the devil's direct involvement! Here is the continuum: desire, entrapment, desire conceived, which gives birth to sin, and when the seed of sin is fully grown, it produces the fruit of death! (We will discuss Satan's role in another chapter.)

When it comes to the Word of the Kingdom, he is only able to steal it away because of the condition of our hearts, not because he has great power or authority. In fact, all three of the things that keep the Word from growing and producing fruit in our lives are heart conditions.

The first category of people Jesus teaches about in the parable of the Sower are those who experience seed sown by the wayside. The wayside is not actually the heart! The wayside represents a path or road where, because of the traffic, the soil has been packed down and hardened to such a degree that the seed lays on top of the ground and can be easily stolen.

The Immutable Law of the Seed

> *When anyone hears the word of the kingdom and does not understand it, then the wicked one comes and snatches away what was sown in his heart. This is he who received seed by the wayside.* (Matthew 13:19-20)

A casual glance at this passage would initially lead us to believe Satan has direct access to our hearts and is able to steal the Word at his will. The most important thing about the seed in this analogy is that, based on the original language, the seed was not sown in the heart; it was scattered by the wayside.

In Jeremiah 17:9, the KJV of the Bible says, *"The heart is deceitful above all things, And desperately wicked; Who can know it?"*

The phrase "desperately wicked" means to be sick, incurable, and in poor health. The word deceitful means covered with footprints.[17]

Since the heart is incurably ill, God doesn't try to fix it when we get saved. He actually gives us a new heart and a new spirit. But most people have been exposed to hurt, pain, rejection, humiliation, and sorrow to such a degree, like the hardened path from those who walk on it; our hearts are hardened and broken. A hard heart doesn't actually receive the seed.

Interestingly, the phrase "received the seed" shows us something very important. The word that is always used for receiving something by faith means to "take hold and bring it unto oneself." However, this word for "receive" is a passive word, which indicates that the subject allowed something to be done to them. They didn't do anything or make choices. I would liken these people to passive, noncommittal hearers of the Word (James 1:22).

Even more important is that, according to Jesus, a dull or hard heart doesn't allow anything that would present the need for change to be accepted into it. The first requirement for Kingdom living is a repentant heart, i.e., a teachable, flexible, and adaptable heart.

It is essential that we always remember: Satan can only steal from me what I give him opportunity through unbelief, fear, or disobedience. But according to Jesus' teaching on the Keys of the Kingdom, I can stop him any time I choose.

---

17   Satan Unmasked, reveals the authority we have over the devil and frees us from an unjustified fear.

When Satan comes to steal the Word, he uses the same tricks he has always used. He is a liar, deceiver, and an accuser. But it's not him personally whispering in our ears. It is a lifetime of being influenced by the carnal and ungodly. What we learn in school, from our families, and literally from every influence in our lives has come by way of Tares, who have sown their godless message in the world.

When we expose ourselves to the Word of the Kingdom, everything we've heard from religion floods our minds in the form of self-accusation and self-disqualification. He is not whispering in our ears, but we, through our self-talk, are promoting the doctrine of demons, which plants the seed in our hearts.

In future chapters you will discover the biblical process for changing your internal dialog!

Divine Prescriptions

- Take time to ponder what God spoke to you in this chapter.
- Ask Him, "In light of what I'm seeing, what are you speaking to me?"
- Then, "How do I apply what I'm seeing to my life?"
- Regardless of How I personally feel about what you're showing me, "You are my Lord. I am willing to follow your leadership."
- I am willing for you to bring me to the place of trusting and applying everything you speak to me."

13. Seeds on Stony Ground

When the circumstances that compelled us to call on the Lord go away, our commitment to Him also goes away!

The parable that explains the stony ground gives us many insights into the subtle factors about why some people begin to make the journey with God but never follow through. Let's take a look at this part of the parable:

> *These likewise are the ones sown on stony ground who, when they hear the word, immediately receive it with gladness; and they have no root in themselves, and so endure only for a time. Afterward, when tribulation or persecution arises for the word's sake, immediately they stumble.* (Mark 4:16-18)

The first hint we have to understand this group of people is the use of the word "immediately." Notice that they *immediately* received the Word and then they *immediately* began to struggle when they faced opposition or persecution.

Some behavioral types seem to act impulsively, but that doesn't mean they are "flakes." The Apostle Peter was incredibly impulsive, and it did create some difficulties for him. However, his character always caused him to rise above his impulsive mistakes.

I want to focus on the issues that emerge from impulsiveness. But it is important that you don't condemn yourself if you are an impulsive person. God always finds a way to work through our behavioral type, no matter how it might limit us. There is no perfect behavioral type, and there are no bad behavioral patterns. God can work through anyone who is teachable! Always remember, whatever your behavior pattern, it is your character that determines if you will walk in its weaknesses or strengths!

Jesus warned that we all must count the cost of following Him (Luke 14:26-28). Most new converts in the 21st century don't come to Him to become disciples; they come to escape some problem. They have no interest in changing their lives or making any commitment to Lordship. Those are people who have not heard the biblical concept of the Gospel: what happened on the Cross, in the grave, and through the resurrection.

The biblical account of the gospel is the truth that compels a person to recognize the price Jesus paid for their salvation, inspiring them to trust Him enough to confess Him as Lord! Until there is a confession, i.e., a commitment to Lordship, people feel that following Him is an option, only observed when it is convenient or when they are in trouble. Because they didn't make a quality decision about Lordship and count the cost, they can reverse their decision very quickly.

Years of evidence reveal that when the circumstances that compelled us to call on the Lord go away, our commitment to Him also goes away!

Scripture says this person joyfully and immediately receives the word. But this word for receive doesn't mean to "take hold of and bring it unto oneself." The word used in this passage is more of a passive word. As we will discover in the condition required for the seed to take root, there must be a deliberate taking of hold of the Word by faith, which involves cultivating and nurturing the seed.

In this portion of the parable, it is very clear that this person did not count the cost of Kingdom living.

The presence of rocks reveals that they never broke up their fallow ground. They didn't prepare the soil so the seed could take root and flourish.

Matthew 13:5 tells us that *"**some** of the seeds"* that were scattered fell on stony ground. The word some is an important word. The Greek for "some" means "some of the same kind"[18] instead of some of a different kind.

The same quality of seed that was sown among thorns was the same kind that was sown in good ground and brought forth an abundance of fruit.

> UNTIL WE PREPARE OUR HEARTS TO RECEIVE THE SEED, IT WON'T MATTER WHAT WE HEAR OR READ.

Since the word was the same in all four examples, we realize that no matter the quality of the word preached, what matters is the condition of the soil/heart. When we struggle, we tend to think, "I need to get more teaching or read the Bible more." This may be true to some degree. However, until we prepare our hearts to receive the Seed, it won't matter what we hear or read. It won't produce the desired fruit!

It's important to realize our hearts cannot embrace two opposing facts at the same time. We can distinguish the difference, but we can't embrace opposing beliefs. We will always choose one or the other.

The stony ground was full of rocks. The original language indicates that the rocks covered the ground so completely that there was only a thin layer of soil covering them. The rocks may not have even been visible. This looked like any other field.

The soil did make it possible for the seed to take root and begin to grow. But because of the rocks that lay just beneath the surface, they had no way to take root. Therefore, when the sun came up, the weak infant plants were scorched, withered, and died (Matthew 13:6).

Matthew 13:20 says the hearer had *"no root in himself."* This is similar to the seed sown on the wayside, which is another case of the seed not being able to sink roots deep into the soil. Those who have only a superficial relationship with truth and have not permitted it to make its way into the utmost recesses of their being may start well, repeatedly, but it seldom ends well!

---

18   from The Complete Word Study Dictionary: New Testament © 1992 by AMG International, Inc. Revised Edition, 1993

Jesus went on to say, *"For when tribulation or persecution arises because of the word, immediately he stumbles."*

It's interesting to note that their persecution did not arise because they identified as "believers." It arose because of their lack of commitment to the Word.

In the Roman world, it was legal to worship Jesus. The Romans were polytheistic. Nearly every Roman worshiped many gods. However, it was illegal to confess Jesus as Lord. Caesar had to be the absolute Lord over all other gods. The penalty for believing on Jesus as Lord was torture and death!

A person who does not commit to Jesus as Lord is not committed to His Word. Therefore, it is unlikely that this person will ever be persecuted. In their mind, commitment to the Word is optional. It doesn't put them in conflict with those who worship pagan gods. It doesn't affect the way they do business, their morality, or ethics. They fit very comfortably into secular society.

As we see from the issue with the three types of soil that will not allow the seed to grow, there is one common denominator: they never prepared their soil/hearts. They did not begin their journey being repentant and teachable!

Scripture repeatedly tells us to *break up our fallow ground*, i.e., prepare the soil/heart for the Word. If this doesn't happen, it doesn't matter what we are told or what version of the Gospel we hear; we will never understand, believe, receive, or enter into Kingdom Living!

There is one precursor to making a commitment to Jesus. John the Baptist revealed this one factor when he introduced Jesus to the Hebrew world. He said, *"Repent for the Kingdom of heaven is at hand."* (Matthew 3:2) This one factor was so important that Jesus Himself proclaimed the same message immediately upon launching His public ministry (Matthew 4:17).

The Kingdom of God is a realm we enter when we surrender to Jesus' Lordship. But the Kingdom of heaven is a realm where the resources of heaven are available to us in this life.

We are not able to enter the Kingdom of Heaven without first entering the Kingdom of God. In fact, John 3:3 tells us we can't even perceive there is a Kingdom of God unless we are born again. Hearing and receiving the Gospel (the biblical version) has an immediate effect on our hearts, making it possible for us to receive Jesus as Lord, thereby perceiving and entering the Kingdom of God (Lordship.) Lordship prepares our hearts to enter the Kingdom of Heaven (God's resources).

Jesus' parables were, more than any other subject, a look into Kingdom living. Through parables, He brought us face to face with the types of beliefs, attitudes, and fruit one must choose to enter!

The Kingdom is a realm ruled by the King. Lawless, by definition, is one who has no country (government) and no king. As such, he or she has no value or commitment to the laws that govern the Kingdom. In other words, they have no commitment to God's Word.

Those who are not ready to become citizens of the Kingdom and commit to the King have not prepared their hearts to receive the Word of the Kingdom! Keep in mind that this can happen instantly for those who hear and believe the gospel.

Repentance is far more than simply regretting sinful behavior. A repentant heart is one that is ready to change opinions, beliefs, and behaviors for the King and the Kingdom. This person is flexible, adaptable, and teachable.

The preparation for Kingdom living is based on the value one has for the King and the Kingdom. Unfortunately, the church has preached a diluted message of salvation, giving the potential convert no reason to be grateful for what Jesus did.

Remember, until a person hears and believes what happened on the Cross, in the grave, and through the resurrection, they have not heard the Gospel (1 Corinthians 15:3-4).

To the degree you pursue the Lordship of Jesus as expressed in His Word, you will add depth to the soil of your heart. You will develop your heart to the degree that you can hear and maintain the seed you sow, unto good fruit!

Divine Prescriptions

- Take time to ponder what God spoke to you in this chapter.
- Ask Him, "In light of what I'm seeing, what are you speaking to me?"
- Then, "How do I apply what I'm seeing to my life?"
- Regardless of How I personally feel about what you're showing me, "You are my Lord. I am willing to follow your leadership."
- I am willing for you to bring me to the place of trusting and applying everything you speak to me."

14. Seeds Among Thorns

Attempting to hold two opinions simultaneously corrupts them both.

Of all the factors making it impossible for the Word of the Kingdom to grow in our hearts, the most devastating seems to be the thorns. I find the thorns to be a general concept that includes all the things Jesus warned us to avoid: sin, traditions of men, double-mindedness, love of the world, distractions, anxiety, and fellowship with the world are just a few of the things that compete for our attention and choke the Word of God from our hearts.

Our introduction to the *Law of the Seed* starts in Genesis 1:12, *"And the earth brought forth… that yields seed according to its kind."*

Many of the Old Testament Scriptures about practical aspects of life find their ultimate fulfillment in spiritual values expressed in the New Testament.

For example, Deuteronomy 22:9 is one of those warnings that had immediate practical application for farming, but it reaches its ultimate purpose in the New Covenant, *"You shall not sow your vineyard with different kinds of seed, lest the yield of the seed which you have sown and the fruit of your vineyard be defiled."*

The Immutable Law of the Seed

According to Jesus' explanation of the parables, seeds are words, thoughts, opinions, or any type of communication or messaging. The soil is the heart, and the Sower is the one conveying information. It can be someone in your environment conveying information, or it can be your own thoughts and imaginations.

According to Jesus, mixed seeds would be seeds of the Word of The Kingdom and any other seeds, i.e., the philosophies of the World's System. These two types of seeds are diametrically opposed to one another. They will compete for the soil of our hearts just as they compete for space in our gardens.

Because of the sin principle that's in the world and our lifelong obsession with satisfying the lust of our flesh, the weeds, thorns, and thistles tend to grow continuously. On the other hand, it takes diligence and effort to plant and nurture the seed of the Kingdom in our hearts.

I am not talking about the diligence and labor to earn anything from God. The promise is ours because we are in Jesus. Hebrews 4:10-11 says, *"He that is entered into his rest, he also hath ceased from his own works, as God did from his. Let us therefore be diligent (labor) to enter that rest."*

> **LABOR IS NOT WHAT WE DO TO EARN THE PROMISES OF GOD.**

Labor is not what we do to earn the promises of God. We are qualified for all the promises because we are in Christ (2 Corinthians 1:20)! However, the diligent laboring we do is to prepare our hearts to receive and protect the seed.

Jesus taught that once a seed is planted in good soil, it grows without our labor. But our labor is to prepare the soil.

> *The kingdom of God is as if a man should scatter seed on the ground, and should sleep by night and rise by day, and the seed should sprout and grow, he himself does not know how. For **the earth yields crops by itself**.* (Mark 4:26-28)

We must always be diligent in preparing the soil, guarding, and guiding our hearts away from the World's philosophies and into the Word of God. However, due to the overwhelming flood of input from the world, the good seed that produces righteousness is always in danger of having thorns planted in our hearts simply because we are in this world. When we plant those seeds in our hearts, they choke out the Word of God!

This is why Jesus modeled "Foot Washing." Foot washing was a way to remind us that even though we are saved and made righteous through the blood of Jesus, we still get our feet dirty by simply walking through this world. Jesus said if we didn't allow Him to wash our feet, we have nothing in Him. (I'm not referring to the ceremony of foot washing as much as I am referring to the continual need for cleansing of our heart, mind, and conscience.

Let's break down the passage about the thorns.

Matthew 13:22, *"Now he who received seed among the thorns is he who hears the word, and the cares of this world and the deceitfulness of riches choke the word, and he becomes unfruitful."*

Received: once again, this is not the Greek word that means to "take hold and bring it to oneself."

Word: this is a reference to the word of the Kingdom. The fact that the person hears it indicates his intention to put it into practice.

Cares refer to anxiety, distraction, and disruptions to the mind

Of the **World** very obviously points to the wisdom of the world and the lust of the flesh that we seek to fulfill through the world's philosophies (1 John 2:15-17).

Deceitfulness refers to the deceitfulness of sin, thereby becoming delusional and drawn away into the things of the world.

The false hope of **riches:** wealth, possessions, material goods. This can come through greed or fear. Those who live in fear look to wealth for a false sense of security.

Choke is very obviously strangling, drowning, suffocating, overpowering, or replacing the **Word.**

Word: When we lose the Word, we lose the seed. There is no longer any way to bear fruit. We are left spiritually barren: **Unfruitful.**

Of the three types of soil/heart that make it impossible for the Word of Kingdom to come to fruition, there is none as insidious as the seed sown among the thorns.

The hard ground of the wayside and the soil filled with rocks keep the Word from taking root and growing. But the thorns not only choke the Word, but they also produce beliefs and fruit that will destroy our lives. So, as the Word is choked from our hearts, the thorns replace it with worldly, deadly, demonic lies that lay in wait for our blood (Proverbs 12:6)!

Protecting one's heart against the thorns includes preparing the soil, planting the seeds of the Kingdom, and diligently guarding our hearts from input that is contrary to the Word of the Kingdom.

After more than a half-century in ministry, I would say that most believers lose their way because of thorns in the garden of their hearts!

In Proverbs 4:23, we are told to *"keep, guard, and protect our hearts with all diligence."* As straightforward as the directive is, the great majority of believers totally ignore it.

The first problem is that few ministers or laymen have a clue about the heart and how it functions. The second problem is that because of our need for social acceptance, many believers use no biblical discretion concerning what they expose themselves to: television, movies, gossip, slanderers, talebearers, and discord sowers.

The writer of Proverbs asks this question: *"Can a man take fire to his bosom, And his clothes not be burned? Can one walk on hot coals, And his feet not be seared?"* (Proverbs 6:27-28)

The answer to this question is a resounding "No!" We can't violate the wisdom of the Scripture, participate in those things that will defile us, and not have consequences.

If we want Heaven on Earth, we've got to guard our hearts, beginning with who and to what we are exposed.

Divine Prescriptions

- Take time to ponder what God spoke to you in this chapter.

- Ask Him, "In light of what I'm seeing, what are you speaking to me?"

- Then, "How do I apply what I'm seeing to my life?"

- Regardless of How I personally feel about what you're showing me, "You are my Lord. I am willing to follow your leadership."

- I am willing for you to bring me to the place of trusting and applying everything you speak to me."

15. Seeds In Good Soil

Good seed in good ground always produces good fruit... effortlessly!

According to Jesus, the seed is not just the Word of God in general; it is the Word of the Kingdom (Matthew 13:19). In fact, nearly all of the parables are about Kingdom living, even when they don't explicitly say it!

The Greek "word" used in this verse comes from "Logos." While "logos has vast implications. We know that Jesus was the logos made flesh. It is the living word. It is what the word looks like in practical application. Rather than teaching *"line upon line,"* Jesus taught and modeled what it looked like to apply God's word from His motives and intentions.

When we are born again, we receive a new heart and a new Spirit, resulting in the capacity to perceive the Kingdom, John 3:3. The heart is soft, pliable, and teachable. In other words, it is ready to receive the Word of the Kingdom.

There are, however, things that can very quickly render their new heart incapable of seeing, perceiving, or hearing the Word of the Kingdom. The seven parables in the book of Matthew, starting with The Parable of the Sower, all reveal qualities that must be present if we actually intend to hear, understand, and live the logos, just as Jesus did! A commitment to those qualities is an excellent way to prepare our hearts to receive the Word/logos.

It all starts with the issue of Lordship. Lordship implies that Jesus is **your** King. It acknowledges that we have entered His kingdom, and we must follow His leadership.

If one does not make a conscious decision to follow Jesus as Lord, one can enter a state of lawlessness. When someone is lawless, they have no king or government, so they make their own rules.

When we come to walk with Jesus, the first priority of the new birth is to begin the process of renewing our minds! If we don't renew our minds, we continue thinking the way we have always thought. Consequently, our new heart is refilled with seeds that produce thorns, the same thorns that have been there all our lives. Having a heart full of thorns means we continue to think and live much like we always have. These thorns choke out the Word of the Kingdom. Consequently, our journey with God becomes powerless and burdensome.

Remember, the "Word" is the Logos, i.e., the way we live and the path we walk! When the Logos is choked out, we don't merely lose information about the Kingdom; we lose any intention to live as Jesus lived! We become indifferent to how we live.

This is why it's crucial that every believer is developed as a disciple, not a disciple of the church or a leader, but a disciple of the Lord Jesus Christ.

Our life as a disciple is a life of continuous transformation. We don't need transformation because of what's wrong with us. We need transformation so we can share in our inheritance in Christ!

As I have already mentioned, we are *"predestined to be conformed to the image of His Son, that He might be the firstborn among many brethren."* (Romans 8:29)

Before the world was created, before man came on the scene, before sin entered in, God had already determined that Jesus would be glorified as the firstborn from the dead when we jointly enter into His transformation process. It starts on the Cross, where He became our sin. In the grave, He suffered our penalty. Having become our sin, He was held captive in death and the power of sin. In the resurrection, He conquered the power of sin, death, and all principalities and powers!

Learning to put off the old man, renew the mind, and put on the new man created in the image of Christ should begin with water baptism. When we are plunged into the water, we acknowledge that all that we have ever been outside of Jesus has died and is buried. We bury him in a watery grave; we don't try to clean him up; we don't try to fix him with counseling. But we put on the new man when we come up out of that grave. In this, we acknowledge that we are raised with Him into newness of life!

Water baptism is the place where we start the process of renewing our minds. This is where we realize we are in Jesus and have become one with His transformation from becoming our sin (the Cross), dying with Him (the grave), and being raised up in the newness of life (the resurrection).

The teaching that should prepare the new believer for this experience is the Gospel according to God's Word: what happened on the Cross, in the grave, and through the resurrection (1 Corinthians 15:1-4).

This essential process, which the church has minimized for centuries, prepares the soil/heart to receive the Word of the Kingdom. Now that they have a King, they can understand that there is a kingdom. This is the key that unlocks the mysteries of the Kingdom.

Since they are ready to hear the Word of God in their hearts, and they have a deep love and appreciation for Him, their hearts are ready.

The traits of a good heart/soil that can hear and understand start with the New Birth, which makes them capable of perceiving the Kingdom; John 3:3, then biblical discipleship equips them to hear and understand.

Matthew 13:23 says, *"But he who received seed on the good ground is he who **hears** the word and **understands** it, who indeed **bears fruit** and produces: some a hundredfold, some sixty."*

The Greek for "good" refers to something that is valuable, complete, healthy, harmonious, and a suitable place.[19]

---

19 The Complete Word Study Dictionary: New Testament © 1992 by AMG International, Inc. Revised Edition, 1993)

One of the most common things I hear from people who do not read their Bible is, "I don't read my Bible because I can't understand it!" According to Jesus, an inability to understand starts with issues of the heart. This means we should all ask the question, "Is my heart a suitable place to plant the seed of the Kingdom?"

This begs the question, what could make my heart unsuitable to hear and understand the Word of the Kingdom? The answer is simple. We find the answer to our question by asking another question. "Is my heart ready to have a King and live as a citizen in His Kingdom?" Until this issue is settled, understanding will elude us.

WHEN JESUS IS OUR KING/LORD, WE HAVE NOTHING TO HOLD BACK FROM HIM.

When Jesus is our King/Lord, we have nothing to hold back from Him. When we know the price He paid for our salvation, we know He is good and only good. Therefore, we have no fear of what He may ask of us.

But what if there is some part of our life that we hold back from Him? What if there is something we are unwilling to deal with or change? This changes everything. The Hebrew phrase "hear and obey" represents a continuum. It implies that anything we would not be willing to obey, we can never hear, understand, or become willing to obey.

Jesus taught in parables so those who have the heart for it will hear and understand. Those who are unwilling to hear will never understand. He is not causing them to be confused; it is the making of their own hearts. He makes it clear that they are the ones who make themselves incapable of hearing and understanding. Matthew 13:14 says, *"And in them the prophecy of Isaiah is fulfilled, which says: 'Hearing you will hear and shall not understand, And seeing you will see and not perceive.'"*

This describes the state of those who do not hear and understand. It is like walking through a war zone, deaf and blind, with no comprehension of why it's all happening. Matthew 13:15 says:

> *For the hearts of this people have grown dull. Their ears are hard of hearing, And their eyes **they have closed**, Lest they should see with*

*their eyes and hear with their ears, Lest they should understand with their hearts and **turn**, So that I should heal them.*

This explains why they are deaf, blind, and unable to understand. It is a choice they make lest they should be confronted with change.

Verse 15 ends with Jesus presenting the fact that He would heal them, open their eyes, soften their hearts, and make them able to understand if they would give up one thing. Herein is the problem. They want what they have more than they want Kingdom living.

Then, we find the real reason why they choose to remain in this condition. If they heard and understood, they would recognize the call to obedience. Once a person hears and understands, they are compelled by their own heart to "turn."

The Greek for "turn" has a pretty broad concept. The verb has such varied meanings as to convert, to turn, or to change.[20] When people don't get the healing they need, we are quick to accuse them of unbelief. But for many who do not get healed, it is due to what is called secondary gain. In other words, there are some benefits they experience because of their "affliction."

They do have a belief problem, but it is not a lack of faith in healing. Healing is the one thing they are afraid of. Getting healed means changing! It means giving up something that we trust more than we trust God and His ways.

Their faith problem concerns God's goodness. They don't believe God has a way to meet their needs. Therefore, they stay in their situation to keep getting the benefits. They are getting something they want more than healing.

When the seed is sown in good ground, i.e., ground that has prepared to receive the seed, the process of transformation begins. It is painless, permanent, positive, and effortless.[21]

---

20   Theological Dictionary of the New Testament, abridged edition, Copyright © 1985 by William B. Eerdmans Publishing Company. All rights reserved.)

21   https://heartphysics.com/

Divine Prescriptions

- Take time to ponder what God spoke to you in this chapter.
- Ask Him, "In light of what I'm seeing, what are you speaking to me?"
- Then, "How do I apply what I'm seeing to my life?"
- Regardless of How I personally feel about what you're showing me, "You are my Lord. I am willing to follow your leadership."
- I am willing for you to bring me to the place of trusting and applying everything you speak to me."

16. Be Careful What you Hear

The words we hear can alter the course of our lives, be careful what you hear!

In Mark 4:24, in the middle of some wonderful promises, Jesus utters a phrase that is both instructional and an ominous warning. This statement is comprised of multiple warnings. First, we should be careful what we expose ourselves to. Second, we should be careful about how we manage what we hear. These are the two situations where we make ourselves most vulnerable. Guarding against what we hear and what we do with what we hear!

Here are several legitimate ways to translate His warning. As we can see, there are warnings for both what we expose ourselves to and what we do after we hear something!

- Mark 4:24, *"Take heed what you hear."*
- Mark 4:24, *"Consider carefully what you hear."* NIV
- Mark 4:24, *"Be careful what you are hearing."* AMP
- Mark 4:24, *"Keep ever a watchful eye on what you are hearing."* Wuest

He once again brings all things back to the context of the heart when He says, *"He who has ears to hear, let him hear!"* (Mark 4:9)

> EVERYTHING WE HEAR AND SEE HAS THE POTENTIAL TO CHANGE OUR BELIEFS AND ALTER OUR LIVES, FOR GOOD OR BAD.

Why should we be so careful about what we hear? Everything we hear and see has the potential to change our beliefs and alter our lives, for good or bad.

As I have previously stated in this book. Adam's failure that will end in global destruction didn't begin when he believed the lies of the wicked one. No! His failure began when he was willing to have a conversation with him. He wasn't careful about who he listened to!

His willingness to have a conversation with a liar was when he stopped guarding his heart! Likewise, when we involve ourselves with slanderers, gossips, talebearers, or negative "dream stealers," we ignore the admonition to guard our hearts.

I find that most of what I share with people is something they already know in their hearts. I just help them put words and Scriptures to what God has been speaking to them. However, because they were willing to listen to people who contradicted what God was saying to them, they never actually realized the truth.

One of the Greek words for sin is "to hear amiss." This means to hear, but then, for whatever reason, not hold on to it! When we feel that God is speaking to our hearts, our first response should be to go to the Bible to ensure that it is congruent with Scripture.

In the parable of the Sower, the seed is sown on the hardened pathway, Jesus says, the devil, like birds eating seeds that lay on top of the soil, steals the Word. Our concepts of the devil are so unscriptural that we think he can forcibly steal the Word from us, and we have no recourse.

In the chapter on Propagation, we learned that most of the work of the devil is not him personally. It is the tares, the people who repeat doctrines of demons, "water down" the Scripture, teach the traditions of men, or anything else that corrupts the truth. When we hear these things in our schools, pulpits, from government leaders, those who teach false science, and even our families, those words go inside us and lie in wait for our blood (Proverbs 12:6)! At the opportune time, those words come back to our conscious thoughts and steal what God is attempting to do in our lives. This usually occurs through our self-talk!

Instead of thinking about the devil through the paradigm of religion and superstition, we could better understand how he operates by simply looking at the meaning of his name. His name means liar, false accuser, and slanderer. He accused God and influenced one-third of the angels to rebel. He accused God and seduced Adam and Eve. He always begins by slandering God, which is what we hear from all these destructive sources. Once we begin to question God, we move to self-accusation.

I contend that one of the primary reasons we hear amiss, i.e., let the Word of God slip from us, is that we condemn ourselves. He's not there whispering in our ears, but the voices of the wicked, or those who, through unbelief, undermine our confidence in God, are in us, waiting for the moment they can steal what God is attempting to do in our lives.

In the previous chapter, we saw that the law of Sowing and Reaping causes those who have to get more and those who have not to lose what little they have left!

When we willfully listen to the words of a gossip or slanderer, we are expressing something, an issue that exists in our own hearts!

This reveals an interesting aspect of God's ethics. He doesn't promise people equal outcomes; that is up to the hearer. But He does promise that we all start with the same resources: the Scriptures, the Holy Spirit, and the freedom to choose. If God made the decision about who will live in blessings and who will live in curses, it would be a violation of our will, i.e., freedom of choice.

Some interpret this verse to say God will give more to one and take away from another. But the truth is, the person who is growing a good crop in his heart just keeps expanding the blessings. God is not making an arbitrary decision about this. It is the *Immutable Law of the Seed*. When we sow good seed in good soil, it produces good fruit! We get more of what we have in our hearts!

The Immutable Law of the Seed

In the English Old Testament, there are phrases that are often translated as God taking action or causing certain things to happen. However, many times, the Hebrew reveals that God took no action to produce the outcome. No! The good or bad outcome, the blessing or the cursing, is based entirely on the *Law of the Seed*. People who sow to the flesh reap of the flesh. If they sow to Spirit, they reap of the Spirit (Galatians 6:7-8). Why does that happen? The *Immutable Law of the Seed* says, "Every seed produces after its own kind." It is impossible to sow a seed that produces a crop different than the seed. We get more of the same kind of seeds that are in our hearts unless we repent and become teachable.

If we take the phrase "be careful what we hear" as a warning, we realize the power of hearing. Hearing and seeing are gateways that eventually lead to the heart. Hearing and seeing are seeds that, once seen, we cannot unsee, or once heard, we cannot unhear!

If we do not guard our hearts from specific kinds of input, we risk becoming emotionally and spiritually compromised.

We've all had a lifetime of unscriptural and even antichrist doctrine deposited in our hearts. Many times, it is from those we love and respect. Too often, it is well-meaning people who think they are helping. But we cannot love, trust, and respect them more than we love, trust, and respect God!

Divine Prescriptions

- Take time to ponder what God spoke to you in this chapter.
- Ask Him, "In light of what I'm seeing, what are you speaking to me?"
- Then, "How do I apply what I'm seeing to my life?"
- Regardless of How I personally feel about what you're showing me, "You are my Lord. I am willing to follow your leadership."
- I am willing for you to bring me to the place of trusting and applying everything you speak to me."

17. The Multiplication Factor

No seed bears just one seed, they can bring forth hundreds of seeds!

One of the misunderstood aspects of the *Immutable Law of the Seed* is the multiplication factor. The Law of Multiplication tells us that the seed has the potential to produce thirty, sixty, or even a hundredfold return.

This staggering fact should be a wake-up call for how we manage our thoughts and guard our hearts. I am convinced that for most serious believers, the greatest snare is planting more thorns in their hearts than seeds of the Kingdom.

According to biblical definition, every conversation, including complaining, gossiping, worrying, imagining, remembering, pondering, and considering, is a form of meditation. Meditation occurs when we experience something as being real in this moment.

Proverbs 18:21 emphasizes the need to guard our words and our hearts from the words we hear, *"Death and life are in the power of the tongue, and they who indulge in it shall eat the fruit of it [for death or life]."* (AMP)

In the early 1970s, many charismatics believed that if we merely spoke something negative, it would come back on us like a curse. It seemed that people believed spoken words just floated around until an opportune time came to attack us.

While I absolutely believe we should set watch over our mouths, we should consider all our words and all our communication.

> **THE REAL DANGER OF SPEAKING WORDS IS WHEN THEY ARE HEARD, AND THE HEARER PONDERS THEM.**

The real danger of speaking words is when they are heard, and the hearer ponders them. This is made clear in the following passage. *"Like a madman who throws firebrands, arrows, and death, Is the man who deceives his neighbor And says, 'I was only joking.'"* (Proverbs 26:18-19)

These words did not hurt his neighbor just because they were spoken but because they were spoken and heard. We have to consider what our words do in the hearts of the hearer. In guarding our hearts, we have to ask, what do things I say and listen to do to my own heart?

Whether the spoken words brought chaos or peace, light or darkness, edification or chaos, when we hear them and begin to reflect on them, we are planting seeds that reproduce after their own kind and multiply in the process. Words can work for our good or our destruction based on the quality of the seed and the condition of our hearts! Whether good or bad,

Consider this! The average ear of corn has around 800 kernels, with one to three ears per stalk, depending on the type of corn. This means there could be as many as 2400 kernels yield for each seed planted. Jesus said it like this, *"...whoever has, to him more will be given, and he will have abundance."* (Matthew 13:12)

One seed with a twenty-four hundred return represents a massive multiplication. Seeds are words, whether thought or spoken, including intentions. Those seeds are nurtured by the degree of thought, pondering, considering, imagination, study, and meditation we give them. Any seed based on fear, when planted and nurtured, will grow hundreds more thoughts and feelings of fear, or maybe the intensity of our fears will

The Multiplication Factor

multiply hundreds of times. The growth of our fears, lusts, greed, or emotional pain is not a personal attack of the devil; it is an assault by our own hearts and minds because of what we have allowed ourselves to hear, speak, and think about!

When we speak words, they may seem innocent and harmless, but the way the mind works is that we reinforce the things we believe simply by saying them.

The mind always seeks to protect our ego by causing us to perceive things in a way that confirms our words and opinions. Once we've spoken, the mind goes to work to convince us that it is true and real, i.e., we are right. Everyone who has told a lie can attest to the fact that the more we say it, the more convinced we become that it's true.

This is why we must consider the conversations we have, whether we are doing the talking or listening. Of course, the most powerful conversation we'll ever have is with ourselves via our internal dialog.

If we have any intention of living a life that bears fruit, we must *"Keep and guard your heart with all vigilance and above all that you guard, for out of it flow the springs of life."* (Proverbs 4:21 AMP)

The great news is that, although we tend to suffer from the corrupt things written on our hearts, it's just as easy to develop our hearts in love, righteousness, and all the positive character traits. In upcoming chapters, we will learn that once we sow the seed, it grows by itself to bring forth the fruit of our faith!

If the thoughts of our minds and meditations of our hearts are on that which builds us up, the law of multiplication works for us. That's why the Apostle Paul said,

> *Whatever things are true, whatever things are noble, whatever things are just, whatever things are pure, whatever things are lovely, whatever things are of good report, if there is any virtue and if there is anything praiseworthy—meditate on these things.* (Philippians 4:8-9)

When we utilize the Immutable Law of the seed, spiritual, emotional, and even physical healing and growth can occur very rapidly!

Divine Prescriptions

- Take time to ponder what God spoke to you in this chapter.

- Ask Him, "In light of what I'm seeing, what are you speaking to me?"

- Then, "How do I apply what I'm seeing to my life?"

- Regardless of How I personally feel about what you're showing me, "You are my Lord. I am willing to follow your leadership."

- I am willing for you to bring me to the place of trusting and applying everything you speak to me."

18. The Measure You Meet

We always get more of what we've got unless we change the input that gets into our hearts!

The word "measure," as used in the parable of the Seed, is just that—a measurement, quantity, or portion. It refers to the amount of effort we put into nurturing the Word we hear, which will determine what we get from it.

This sounds like a contradiction of grace, i.e., God's power to do the work. That's because receiving based on the measure we put into something is a paradox. We are only seeking to receive that which God has already given. We are not attempting to persuade Him to give us something that is not already provided in Jesus.

All miracles are instantaneous—once faith is activated in our hearts! However, arriving at the place to receive them instantaneously is a process of nurturing the seed and the soil. That is where we put forth the effort, i.e., the measure of effort.

The book of Hebrews discusses the children of Israel's call to enter the Promised Land in great detail. Unfortunately, many believe the promised land is heaven after we die. No! The Promised Land is a realm we enter into in this life where we share in God's promises and provisions. Some would say this is a type of the Kingdom of Heaven, i.e., a realm where the resources of heaven are available to us now!

However, to understand this, we must resolve yet another paradox. *"For he who has entered His rest has himself also ceased from his works."* (Hebrews 4:10). Canaan is a type of the Kingdom of Heaven.

> **WHEN BELIEVERS ENTER INTO REST, THEY CEASE FROM THEIR OWN LABORS AND EXPERIENCE GOD'S POWER WORKING IN AND THROUGH THEM!**

Entering the Kingdom of Heaven is tantamount to entering into rest. When believers enter into rest, they cease from their own labors and experience God's power working in and through them! These parables of the Seed as the Word of the Kingdom show us how to stop depending on our power and strength and begin experiencing the power of God!

Even though we are entering into rest, it is preceded by labor. *"Let us, therefore, be diligent (labor) to enter that rest."* (Hebrews 4:11-12) The measure we put into the Word we hear is the labor that leads to rest. It is not labor to earn something from God.

I call this effort "Persuading the Heart." Abraham walked into the promise and purpose God had for his life; he dealt with personal failures and continuous setbacks. But he had a secret skill. When he began to waver, he would go back to God and persuade, i.e., fully convince his heart that the promise was true because God was faithful.

> *He did not waver at the promise of God through unbelief, but was strengthened in faith, giving glory to God, and being fully convinced (persuaded) that what He had promised He was also able to perform.* (Romans 4:20-21)

This persuading his heart would recover him when he began to doubt. This was the measure he put into the Word he was hearing! Which eventually brought him to a place of rest. In other words, we labor to persuade our hearts, but when we become "fully convinced," there is no longer a need to put forth that kind of effort.

Coming to the "rest" of faith can be quite challenging. In our modern world, developing this skill of entering into rest is very different from what it was for the people of Jesus' day!

The people Jesus taught knew the Scripture. Even though they had a corrupt interpretation, they still had a workable knowledge of God's Word. When Jesus demonstrated what the Word looked like in real life, it was very easy for them to come to repentance about their beliefs and opinions because they recognized the fulfillment of Scripture in His lifestyle. Thus, they saw the Word manifest in the flesh.

Today, we face a different set of obstacles. Very few believers have a working knowledge of the Scripture. Their beliefs are a hodgepodge of scriptures taken out of context. Add that to 2000 years of occult teaching woven into Christian doctrine, and don't forget the fact that everything in public education is designed to destroy our faith.

People have asked me to explain why I saw so many miracles and healings on the mission field but relatively few in America. It's simple! When our hearts are overgrown with thorns, i.e., that which opposes the truth, the Word we hear is choked out before it can bring forth fruit!

Coming to faith can be confusing and overwhelming. Faith is when we are sure of what we hear (Hebrews 11:1). Faith is also present tense. There is much confusion about understanding the difference between hope and faith.

Hope is the predecessor of faith. Hope looks to the future, with the expectation of the promise coming to pass. Faith, on the other hand, experiences the promise as if it has already happened. Paul explains this distinction in Romans 8:24, *"Hope that is seen is not hope; for why does one still hope for what he sees?"*

When we have hope, we are sure something **is going** to happen. Faith, however, is when a promise of God is experienced as being real in this very moment! This is when we experience it as having already happened!

Sadly, as the early church became increasingly secular, its primary goal became controlling the laity. Therefore, it had to do everything possible to disempower the average believer. Consequently, all true spiritual aspects of the gospel were left out of church doctrine. They didn't want anyone to be able to connect with God without going through the clergy. Nearly all the tools and methods God provided to help us persuade and establish our hearts were buried and, in some cases, outlawed!

Rest is the place where we stop nurturing (measuring) the seed because we know it is settled in heaven and in our hearts. We have experienced the promise as real in our hearts, and we are sure we will experience it in the physical world! The time it takes to make this journey, from hearing the promises to bearing fruit, is determined by how quickly we can fully persuade our hearts.

It is the time between hearing and producing fruit that we labor to persuade our hearts. When our hearts are fully persuaded, we cease from our labor and enter into rest.

When speaking of this rest, the writer of Hebrews says, *"Therefore, since a promise remains of entering His rest."* That there are continued mentions about entering into rest reveals that the "rest" didn't end with the sabbath rest or entering into Canaan. There is a rest for every believer today. Thus, we have another warning, *"…let us fear lest any of you seem to have come short of it. For indeed the gospel was preached to us as well as to them …"*

The word "fear" has a pretty varied meaning. It can mean to be frightened, to be alarmed, to be in awe, even cause to run away. These and other feelings of dread and disappointment will dominate our lives if we do not find this place of rest where the Word bears fruit. *"But the word which they heard did not profit them, **not being mixed with faith** in those who heard it."*

The children of Israel could not enter into God's promises because they did not fully trust Him. Through their unbelief, they limited God (Psalm 78:41-42).

Psalm 78:36 says, *"For their heart was not **steadfast** with Him."* This Scripture reveals that the root of their problem was that their hearts were not fully persuaded; therefore, it was impossible for them to be steadfast!

*"For **we who have believed do enter that rest**."* (Hebrews 4:1-3)

When we operate in true biblical faith, we find our way into the "rest of God!" Our labors are over when we persuade our hearts to believe the truth. Our labors don't make the seed grow; they don't make the miracle happen. But a heart filled with faith, i.e., trust for God, sustains the seed that brings forth the fruit.

When we hear a Word that resonates with our hearts, the first thing we should do is seek God for a Divine Prescription, i.e., a plan for application. The exercises at the end of each of these chapters are the most functional way to learn to hear God's voice while receiving God's wisdom for our situation.

Divine Prescriptions

- Take time to ponder what God spoke to you in this chapter.

- Ask Him, "In light of what I'm seeing, what are you speaking to me?"

- Then, "How do I apply what I'm seeing to my life?"

- Regardless of How I personally feel about what you're showing me, "You are my Lord. I am willing to follow your leadership."

- I am willing for you to bring me to the place of trusting and applying everything you speak to me."

19. Harmony With God

Everything about anything gives us an understanding of all things!

All of creation reveals the character and nature of God. Unless we accept the false teaching of occult groups or "buy into" the theories of false science, everything God has created will teach us about him! Additionally, it will give us insight into all of creation!

In this age of "specialists," we have lost one of the most important spiritual concepts: harmony! When a person becomes a specialist, they tend to lose their awareness of the whole. They are, in fact, trained to narrow their focus. They lose the ability to harmonize all the pieces into one congruent whole.

For example, politicians who have never worked outside of government or run a business have no clue about the needs of the average man. They do not understand the economy, taxes, and, ironically, the laws that would create a fair and just society. They are idealists with little connection to reality! They seldom connect the dots on any of the laws they pass or the effects that law has on the country as a whole. They only see how it will benefit their special interest groups while destroying the rest of the country! Politicians are specialists at one thing—getting elected!

Doctors who become specialists often lose their sense of how the body works together as one system! They treat one area of the body sometimes with no regard or knowledge of how that treatment affects the rest of the body.

> **MINISTERS WHO BECOME SPECIALISTS VIOLATE THE ADMONITION TO PREACH AND TEACH THE WHOLE COUNSEL OF GOD!**

Ministers who become specialists violate the admonition to preach and teach the *whole counsel of God!* They tend to have their doctrinal preferences leading to one-dimensional solutions that never fully produce what is promised. For example, a "faith preacher" will tend to make faith the total solution for all problems. A preacher who embraces deliverance will think deliverance is the cure-all. Specialist preachers attempt to make everything in the Bible about their "pet doctrine."

When we break the Scriptures up into non-related passages and categories, we lose sight of the fact that the Scriptures are about Jesus. He can't be divided. It is impossible to capitalize on one Scriptural passage and remain in harmony with the living Word: Jesus the Christ!

Many of the great cultures of the world produce some of the best thinkers, philosophers, and problem solvers who study many different arts/crafts/skills/subjects. This gives them a broader worldview. Even the apostles who turned the world upside down with the Gospel were fishermen, tent makers, shepherds, and farmers! Their varied life experience gave them a more holistic understanding of the world.

The wider the scope of what we know, the more it opens our understanding of all things. On the other hand, specializing in one area tends to render us myopic and incapable of seeing the big picture.

Much of the disorder in our world can be attributed to the emergence of specialists who focus on one aspect of a situation while remaining blind to the full picture. In our ego-driven world, we attempt to make our "specialist point of view" the solution to all our woes! This produces chaos, conflict, and the most deceptive kind of disorder: our inability to think beyond one-dimensional concepts and solutions.

When we do not see humans as spirit, soul, and body, we may help them in one area while doing great damage to another. This idealistic mentality leads to physical, spiritual, and emotional disharmony: the inability to bring the many pieces together and see it as a whole. This ability is what the Bible calls "understanding." According to Jesus, no matter how great the preaching and teaching we receive, without understanding, it will never bear fruit. Likewise, without understanding, we will never see how the pieces all harmonize.

Based on the principle of the logos, every word in the Bible is connected to and influenced by every other word in the Gospel.

One key to reading and understanding the Bible is learning to recognize patterns. One-dimensional thinkers have great difficulty identifying patterns. The Bible is a complete thought. Based on the principle of the Logos, every Word in the Bible is related to every other word in the Bible. As long as we grasp God's full counsel about any matter, there are no conflicts or contradictions. However, there are paradoxes!

Paradoxes are not contradictions; they are "seeming contradictions." This is where a healthy, teachable heart first reveals itself. In the parable of the Sower, we are told that one of the key roles of the heart starts with understanding. The word for "understanding" in the Original Greek refers to bringing all the pieces together. This is when it becomes obvious that what we previously saw as a contradiction in Scripture is a paradox that can only be grasped by the heart, not the intellectual mind! Until we bring all the pieces together, we cannot identify the patterns; the understanding of the Word evades us.

There is an ancient saying, "As above, so beneath." This saying refers to the microcosm and macrocosm. The macrocosm could be the entire universe, while the microcosm could be an atom. The number of atoms that make up the universe would be beyond our ability to calculate. But we can look at the observable universe and see how every single atom serves to make up the whole. These atoms must be in harmony; otherwise, there would be no coherent universe. It would be total chaos.

The human body is a macrocosm; its cells are the microcosm. Likewise, all the organs and components that make up the human body are microcosms of the human being.

When God created the heavens, the Earth, and all that exists therein, He observed the law of harmony: the macrocosm-microcosm! In other words, all things are in harmony. All things follow patterns that emerge from God's heart and are expressed in Scripture. These things open our understanding to all other things in creation.

This means there is an obvious harmony between the functioning of all things. Once we understand how one thing in creation works, we can understand how all things in the creation work. Thus, my saying: *Everything about anything gives us an understanding of all things!*

The specialists have accurately observed many different aspects of creation. But until they look at all the pieces as one harmonized whole, they will never fully understand creation. However, their greatest limitation to understanding is because they have made the choice not to "perceive God," the Creator. They chose not to understand; they chose not to see God. Why? If they perceived God, they would have to repent of their wicked ways and change (Romans 1:20-23). They do not want to change, so they have, by default, chosen not to see God in Creation.

From this ego-driven place of false science, they develop theories that there is no way to prove. They convince us that creation is the result of chaos, organizing itself, apart from intelligence. Once we become confused or deceived about creation, we, too, begin to see the world as segregated events and pieces of information that have no harmony with anything else in the universe. When this happens, the Law of Harmony is forsaken, and our capacity for understanding is diminished!

"Tares" are the product of corrupt seeds in our hearts in the form of words, theories, and concepts. Since we accept them as true, their seed fills our hearts with thorns that choke our capacity to hear the word, understand, and bear fruit!

The Greek word "logos" directly refers to Jesus. It is a reference to the Living Word, i.e., what the Word of God looks like in real life! The concept of logos is vast, but it holds a secret to developing an understanding heart!

Among many other things, logos can be understood as *"the Way."* Jesus called Himself the "way." He showed us the way of God. In Acts 9:2, believers were called those who were of *the Way*! The word "way" is another comprehensive word. As much as anything, in biblical context, it refers to those who follow "a way of life." Since Jesus is the way, this would mean the way of life, faith, and godliness that Jesus Himself followed. But it is more than imitating Jesus; it is about entering into Him and harmonizing with Him as one life! The more we harmonize with Him, the more we manifest the logos of God to the world!

As the Creator, all of creation is in harmony with who He is. This means that all creation follows a path, a logic, i.e., the way! Proverbs 12:28 refers to the way of life. It states that in this way, *"there is life and no death."*

If God has established a way or a path wherein there is life and no death, it would seem that walking that path or following that way should be our goal. However, because of 2000 years of religious influence, the average believer would turn this into some type of religious and very possibly legalistic concept. However, those who grasp the concept of harmony will find it to be *easy and light.*

When Jesus said we should take His yoke, He was not referring to taking on a burden—just the opposite. He was referring to harmonizing with Him and where He is walking. When animals are yoked together, the burden is lightened for all who pull the same load. Yoking up with Him doesn't make our journey more burdensome; it makes it easier!

When we walk with Jesus, we don't try to force Him onto the path we choose; we "get in step" with Him; we walk the path He has chosen. This is not done by carnal determination and raw willpower. This is a work of grace! Likewise, all of our endeavors would then be pursued from the perspective of sustaining our Harmony with Him!

Since this way of righteousness (Proverbs 12:28) has life and no death, we can realize a dimension of faith that we may have never considered!

As previously mentioned, the general concept of faith is when we choose a path, i.e., a way we think we will get what we want, but it's out of harmony with who God is and the way He functions. When we experience chaos, pain, and conflict on the path we have chosen, we then operate in what we consider to be faith. We start calling on God to leave the path of life and walk the crooked path we are walking. This is not us harmonizing with God; this is us calling on God to depart from His way and harmonize with our way. The problem is—He only walks on the path of righteousness.

If God intervened to solve our problem, He would be a codependent enabler. It would create the false illusion that there is no reason to walk in His way!

Don't misunderstand; God always wants to meet our needs. He is, after all, the God of "yes"! Paul pointed out that the Gospel He preached was not *yes and no*! It was, yes! God's answer to our every need is, *"Every promise He has ever made to anyone is yes and amen to us because we are in Christ Jesus."* (2 Corinthians 1:19-20)

God's solution to our problems is not to leave His path, step onto our corrupt path, meet our needs, and then repeat that process over and over again. He says, "Yes," I will meet the need. Then He calls us to walk in, i.e., harmonize with Him, because it is in that way, i.e., that path where there is only life and no death.

> **FAITH IS BEING SURE OF WHAT GOD HAS SAID AND DONE.**

Even though I have already made this statement, it bears repeating: Faith is not believing that we can convince God to do our bidding and walk our path. Faith is not confidence in what we think God will do. Faith is being sure of what God has said and done. When He says there is life and no death in His way, that is our call to harmonize with His way!

Instead of working against the "Way" things were created to flow, we can harmonize with how He created things to work. Therefore, the burden is always easy, and the yoke is always light. We put ourselves in a place where abundant life flows.

Jesus, the "logos," is the Creator of all things, Colossians 1:16. And He continues to uphold all things by the Word of His power, Hebrews 1:3! If we believe that our faith is in Him as the Creator, it is also in the way, i.e., logos, by which all of creation works.

All aspects of creation were in harmony with His identity, character, and nature. Therefore, the more we understand creation, the more we can understand God. A person of faith will trust His wisdom and His way of doing things. If we trust Him and harmonize with Him, likewise, we harmonize with His creation. We stop working against God's way to fulfill our dreams and desires, and we get into the flow of His creation and the way it works.

We don't find the word "harmonize" in the Bible, but we are told to yield to righteousness, Walk in the Spirit, become one with Him, abide in Him, and take His yoke. All of these express God's desire for us to harmonize with Him, His character, and nature as revealed in the Word as Jesus taught and applied it!

Divine Prescriptions

- Take time to ponder what God spoke to you in this chapter.
- Ask Him, "In light of what I'm seeing, what are you speaking to me?"
- Then, "How do I apply what I'm seeing to my life?"
- Regardless of How I personally feel about what you're showing me, "You are my Lord. I am willing to follow your leadership."
- I am willing for you to bring me to the place of trusting and applying everything you speak to me."

20. WE ARE WHAT WE DIGEST

Words we hear, like the foods we eat, become part of who we are!

Food becomes a part of who we are through digestion. It has long been said, "We are what we eat." But the truth is, we are what we digest! If food is not metabolized, it is not absorbed into the cells. It doesn't energize our physical body. Food that is not digested, like the Word of God that is not digested, actually produces toxins in our bodies. The word of God that we do not assimilate/digest and put into practice makes us spiritually sluggish and fat.

Based on the macrocosm-microcosm, we can find great insight and hope in this nugget. In the same way, we digest and metabolize foods to become part of who we are, we must digest God's Word for them to become a part of us. This concept can teach us one of the most powerful and simple ways to guard and guide our hearts!

By the way, this isn't just an abstract theoretical concept. When I had my clinic, one of the primary areas we treated was digestive disorders. Since Huntsville has several colleges and various training programs, we very often had college students as clients. The digestive disorders of these students were caused by their academic load.

As it turns out, the same energies used by the body to digest food are the same energies it uses to metabolize mental information. Students most commonly develop serious digestive issues around exams or when working on a thesis or dissertation. As their digestive disorder worsens, their capacity to maintain, manage, and recover information also becomes compromised. After all, thinking is simply metabolizing information!

The great hope we have from observing this microcosm-macrocosm of processing and digesting is that we have confirmation that, just like the foods I consume, if I do not metabolize the things I hear and the things that enter my mind, they do not become part of who I am!

As previously discussed, spoken words don't float around the Globe like an invisible virus that attacks our bodies, bringing sickness! Words, like most viruses, are opportunists. They can only affect us if we hear them, and there is an underlying issue making us vulnerable.

Actually, we have no knowledge of how spoken words affect our world. But we do know how "heard words" affect our hearts!

Words that are "heard" are the words that possess the greatest probability of improving or worsening the quality of our lives. This doesn't mean we must be phobic about the words we hear. In order for the seed to grow, it must be planted in the soil and metabolized. Even falling into sin goes through the same process as "falling into" the promise of God!

Temptation starts with an underlying desire, just like the promise. Then, we are drawn away as we look to the world's system to gratify that desire. With the promise, we look to God, who has already promised to fulfill our needs and desires. In temptation, the next phase is enticement, i.e., entrapment. In the promise, the next phase is being captivated by the promise. The last stage of the temptation-sin syndrome is that through our imagination, sin is conceived. With the promise, through our thought, study, and imagination, the promise is conceived. The final step in the temptation continuum is sin produces some degree of death (destructive quality of life). In the situation of the promise, when it is conceived, it brings life (the life of God).

When we grasp how easy it is to move from temptation to death, we realize how incredibly easy we can move from the promise to the fulfillment.

We Are What We Digest

In every situation, good or bad, we operate according to the *Immutable Law of the Seed*.

We have the power and authority to instantly stop wicked words from having any power in our lives when we stop nurturing them and begin to sow good seeds in our hearts!

Since all things work by the same *Immutable Law of the Seed*, we have proof of this ever-functioning law. Sometimes, when we don't believe we can make it work for us, we can look at some of the destructive areas of our lives and see that it is functioning perfectly!

Divine Prescriptions

- Take time to ponder what God spoke to you in this chapter.
- Ask Him, "In light of what I'm seeing, what are you speaking to me?"
- Then, "How do I apply what I'm seeing to my life?"
- Regardless of How I personally feel about what you're showing me, "You are my Lord. I am willing to follow your leadership."
- I am willing for you to bring me to the place of trusting and applying everything you speak to me."

21. Faith And Patience

It doesn't take special faith to enjoy a supernatural life!

When a believer thinks about experiencing the miraculous, they may have a one-dimensional point of reference. They may believe we should work faith to convince God to take action. After all, the current paradigm is that miracles are always acts of God!

However, as we have discovered, miracles are very often when we operate in higher natural laws that were programmed into creation by the Creator! This is a way of operating faith that is foreign to so many believers.

Two Greek words are translated as "miracle." One of the words refers to something miraculous. The other word, translated as "miracle," comes from the Greek "dunamis," which is normally translated as power. So, the essence of a miracle is a manifestation of power.

Of all the displays of power, there is none more magnificent than the transformation of a human being. A transformed life is far more powerful at glorifying God than a sign or wonder. People can discount or deny the legitimacy of a miracle, but a person who miraculously changes so dramatically that all can see cannot be denied. The proof continues day after day by the quality of their life and emotions.

> **ALL MIRACLES ARE DESIGNED TO DO AT LEAST TWO THINGS: GLORIFY GOD AND MEET THE NEEDS OF THE HUMAN BEING WHO RECEIVES IT!**

Bearing fruit is a miraculous demonstration of the Power (dunamis) of God! Fruit can be the fruit of the Spirit, which manifests in our character. This gives witness to the goodness and mercy of God every day. Fruit could also be an operation of the *gift of miracles* (dunamis). Any influence on the life of a human being is a manifestation of power (dunamis). All miracles are designed to do at least two things: glorify God and meet the needs of the human being who receives it!

When Jesus preached to the Israelites, they were not born again. They had been oppressed by religious legalism for millennials. He came exercising authority as the Son of Man, Matthew 7:29 and John 5:27. He operated in the gifts of the Holy Spirit, just as we do! While Jesus' miracles and healings had a phenomenal impact on their bodies. That was not when or how they experienced transformation. They experienced transformation by believing what He taught and taking it into their hearts.

Because of a works-based mentality, they probably understood very little about the heart. Jesus taught more from the Book of Deuteronomy than any of the Torah. The Book of Deuteronomy, more than any of the Torah, emphasized the need to internalize the word by taking it into the heart. It is the book that emphasizes internalizing, which, up until that time, had only been seen as external behavior. No doubt, His signs and wonders drew them to Him, but the transformations they experienced by His teaching were, very probably, the most persuasive aspect of His ministry.

Those hearers of the Word didn't have the Holy Spirit working in them, and they didn't have the grace of God working in their hearts. So, when they experienced something as powerful as internal transformation, it was abundantly apparent that they were experiencing something greater than they had ever seen or heard! However, they had no clue as to why or how His teachings were so powerful and profound. They just followed His instructions and saw His Teachings come to pass by bearing fruit.

Faith And Patience

To prevent them from engaging in dead religious works, Jesus explained how fruit grows. He had already taught them to ponder, consider, reflect, and meditate on His words, but then He followed up with the most simplistic explanation imaginable.

> *And He said, "The kingdom of God is as if a man should scatter seed on the ground, and should sleep by night and rise by day, and the seed should sprout and grow, he himself does not know how. For the earth yields crops by itself: first the blade, then the head, and after that the full grain in the head. But when the grain ripens, immediately he puts in the sickle, because the harvest has come." (Mark 4:26-29)*

This is an example of the power of typology. He took something they were familiar with to help them understand something that was completely foreign to them.

The statement, "It grows all by itself," reveals the fact that God programmed life into the seed so it would bring forth duplication when placed in a healthy, believing heart!

Bearing fruit is not a product of religious dead works or effort. It is an interaction between the seed and the soil/heart. They understood the laws of farming. They knew all they could do was prepare the soil, plant the seed, and keep the weeds and thorns out, and healthy fruit-bearing crops would be produced with no help from them.

The plague of the 21st-century believer is the need to make it more complicated, more religious, or formula-based. Legalism was the natural pitfall for believers with a Jewish background. But Gnosticism was the primary struggle for Gentile believers.

The heresies of Gnosticism are alive and well in the 21st-century church. We tend to think that the acquisition of information produces miracles instead of simple faith, which is based on the *Immutable Law of the Seed*! Consequently, we put an enormous amount of time and effort into learning new information instead of simply taking the promises that pertain to our needs, sowing them in our hearts, guarding our hearts against the thorns, and abiding in peace as we allow the seed to grow and produce fruit…*all by itself!*

I want to share one more interesting caveat. As the seed germinates, it goes through a growth process. Once it breaks through the ground, it becomes obvious that something is happening. This is when we need to have patience. When we see that first manifestation, we can become discouraged, thinking that the miracle is not what we thought it would be or that maybe this little sprout is all we're going to experience. Unless we begin to feed negative thoughts of unbelief over time, the plant goes through its various stages and finally bears fruit.

Inheriting the promises doesn't occur by faith alone but by faith and patience (Hebrews 6:12).

Functionally, patience is the ability to stand under pressure without wavering. Wavering is when we shift back and forth between two opposing opinions. When we waver, we lose our capacity to receive (take hold of) anything from God (James 1:6-7). God has not rescinded His offer; we just can't take hold of it and sow it into our hearts.

Emotions are the product of where we place our attention. As long as I am focusing on the promise, the seed in my heart is being nurtured. But when my attention is drawn back to the problem, I begin to experience negative, destructive emotions that plant thorns in the garden of my heart. These thorns will choke out the promise that I once experienced.

This is what the Bible calls vain faith. This may be the most confusing and discouraging failure factor of faith. Vain faith starts out truly believing the promise. But it is all in vain; when we waver and begin planting seeds of destruction that choke out the good seed, then we are confused... We know we operated in real faith at the beginning of this journey. So why didn't it come to pass? Simple! We didn't remain patient until the fruit was produced!

We don't have to understand every detail of this process. We must trust the God of Creation enough to follow His process and be patient!

Divine Prescriptions

- Take time to ponder what God spoke to you in this chapter.

- Ask Him, "In light of what I'm seeing, what are you speaking to me?"

- Then, "How do I apply what I'm seeing to my life?"

- Regardless of How I personally feel about what you're showing me, "You are my Lord. I am willing to follow your leadership."

- I am willing for you to bring me to the place of trusting and applying everything you speak to me."

22. Ears To Hear

Hearing is a precursor of faith!

As New Covenant believers, most of us would agree that one of the greatest attributes we should pursue is *sincere faith* (1 Timothy 1:5). Faith is a response of trust in God's character, truthfulness, faithfulness, and dependability!

In the Old Testament, however, faith is only mentioned two times. It is obvious that the principle of faith is paramount to the Old Testament worshiper. As the Old Testament Scripture taught in Habakkuk 2:4, *"The just shall live by faith."* The question we must ask is this, "Is faith an exclusive New Covenant doctrine, or are we missing something about faith?

Jesus' instructions concerning the *Immutable Law of the Seed* repeatedly make reference to "how we hear." In fact, the one exhortation and warning Jesus referred to more than any other is this: *He who has ears to hear…"* Seven times in Matthew and seven times in Revelation, the need to hear is reinforced!

This is one of hundreds of times that we glance at Jesus' teachings and miss the significance of His message. But, on the bright side, this is the perfect example of why we need to be "responsible hearers." Since we hear the Spirit of God in our hearts and not our minds,[22] it doesn't matter if we are reading, listening to something audibly, praying, or meditating. When God speaks, He always speaks in our hearts. Hearing with our heart is the product of a completely different kind of listening.

The Old Testament never denies New Covenant doctrine. Conversely, it always sheds light that makes it easier to grasp and understand every aspect of the New Covenant. This tells us that there is an obvious component of faith and hearing that we are missing.

While the word "faith" is only used two times in the Old Testament, the word "shama," which is translated as "hear," is used 1159 times. Does the word "hear" have any bearing on our understanding of faith? Absolutely! How do we not express the same priority for hearing as the Old Testament Scriptures? And, what are we missing by overlooking this crucial factor?

In Romans 10:17, we're told, *"So then faith comes by **hearing**, and hearing by the word of God."* In this passage, as well as several verses in Hebrews, we discover that hearing precedes faith.[23] It is my belief that the lack of hearing God's voice in our hearts is one of the greatest limiting factors of faith for the majority of believers! This is why the Heart Physics[24] program is so powerful. It helps the believer develop the capacity to hear the voice of God in their hearts!

It seems that New Covenant believers tend to constantly pray that God will speak to them. This type of prayer assumes that God is not attempting to communicate and implies that we have no responsibility in the process.

The concept of "tarrying" was an old Pentecostal concept. People would wait at the altar for God to manifest. To many, this is a sign of faithfulness and integrity on the part of the believer, but it could also be a form of blame-shifting! "OK, God, I'm here; you aren't. I've done my part; you haven't done yours!" I'm listening; you just aren't speaking! Few people would actually accuse God in such a manner, but at the subconscious level, this is the message it is sending!

"I am here, waiting on God, who for some unknowable mystical reason is

Publishing,
23   Hebrew Word Pictures, 2020, Frank T. Seekins, p 192
24   https://heartphysics.com/

waiting until the last minute to "come through for me." This would imply that I am more faithful than God! I'm on time, and He's late, as usual. However, based on the one statement that Jesus repeated more than any other exhortation, *"If anyone has an ear, let him hear."* This would imply that God is already speaking, but we are somehow not hearing!

The Hebrew for the words "hear" and "obey" both come from the Hebrew word "shama". This indicates an intimate link between the two. In the Western mind, we would say that obeying is contingent on hearing, which is a limited reality. In the ancient Hebrew, however, it's just the opposite. Hearing is preceded by the willingness to obey.

Even our ability to understand is linked to our willingness to obey. The idea is this: we will not have the capacity to hear and understand anything we are not already willing to obey! When we desire to hold on to anything outside of Christ, how we hear and understand God will be twisted to our personal preferences.

> **WE WILL NOT HAVE THE CAPACITY TO HEAR AND UNDERSTAND ANYTHING WE ARE NOT ALREADY WILLING TO OBEY!**

When Scripture talks about dying to self, it is not the gruesome suffering that religion has always promoted. "Self" is not the physical man. The physical man's suffering has nothing to do with spiritual development. "Self" is more about our beliefs, opinions, thoughts, and even traditions. What we need to die to is any sense of ourselves, any opinion, belief, or doctrine that is not based on who we are in Christ!

In the parable of the Sower, Jesus makes it obvious that the only way for His Word to bear fruit in our lives is for us to hear and understand. Five different times in the short parable of the Sower, He repeats the need to understand! Understanding is a function of the heart, not the intellectual mind! Understanding begins with knowledge. The repentant, teachable heart brings us to understanding, i.e., the ability to bring all the pieces together and perceive how it all fits into real life. Then wisdom, which comes from the mouth of the Lord, shows us how to apply it for the best outcome (Proverbs 2:6)!

The Immutable Law of the Seed

Wisdom is the practical application of knowledge. It is obedience based on hearing and understanding. It is empowered by the grace of God working in a righteous heart!

In the Hebrew alphabet, there is a unique letter that references God's way of communicating. This is the letter Mem. Mem obviously is used to signify the "M" sound. Mem also represents water, which is a symbol of the mysterious.

One of the mysteries of water is how it affects our perception. When standing in a boat or on a dock looking into the water, the shapes, sizes, and even the location of the things we see in the water are altered. The only way to accurately see and properly perceive what's in the water is to dive in. This is a vague reference to the concept of experiential knowledge, which is the opposite of theoretical knowledge.

But "When," you may ask, "does God speak to us?" The Hebrew language tells us that God speaks to us in at least two definitive ways. He speaks to us through the open Mem, i.e., His revealed knowledge. The revealed knowledge of God is what He has already shown us in creation and said in Scripture. This knowledge is available to anyone who reads and hears what God is saying to them from the Scripture.

Then there is the private or personal knowledge of God, i.e., the closed Mem. This is what God speaks into our hearts as we seek Him. This is the time and place where God shows us how to apply His Word. This is when wisdom comes into our hearts by the mouth of the Lord. This is not God telling you things that are not in Scripture; this is not a private interpretation (2 Peter 1:20). This is the specific personal application of what we have discovered in Scripture.

> **BEING WILLING TO OBEY IS LIKE JUMPING IN THE WATER. ONCE WE ARE COMMITTED TO THE PROCESS, WE "JUMP IN."**

Both of these aspects of how God speaks and leads us require the willingness to obey. Being willing to obey is like jumping in the water. Once we are committed to the process, we "jump in." With that choice, there is almost immediate understanding! But the person who stands in the boat and complains that they don't understand is the person who is actually not willing to understand and obey!

Since we have the Scripture, we can equate that to "God speaking." He is always speaking through His Word! We are never waiting on Him. If we believe the Word is His personal communication with us, we will read and study the Scripture. If we believe He will personally teach us the application of the Word, we will read, pray, and meditate. If we do not believe these two things, we are not in faith; therefore, we cannot hear what the Spirit is saying. We are left without the leadership of the Holy Spirit!

Faith, the willingness to fully trust and give yourself to it, holds nothing back from God. A repentant teachable heart is always ready to leave old opinions, beliefs, and practices behind, i.e., break up the fallow ground! The Holy Spirit can help us to hear, understand, and have the grace to obey. Then the fruit of our lives says, I have heard the voice of the Lord!

In our subconscious attempts at self-justification, we make all of this too difficult. Keep in mind that if our goal is application instead of intellectual interpretation, it becomes incredibly simple!

In Deuteronomy. 30: 11-20 we have the famous *"Choose blessing or curses, life or death"* sermon. It would seem that every person would readily choose life and blessings… and many do. Almost anyone will choose the outcome they desire, but this doesn't mean they have chosen the path that will reach that outcome. Choosing the outcome means nothing if we don't choose the path to reach that outcome. Finding the path, i.e., practical application, occurs when we experience the closed Mem, i.e., God leading us on the path through personal revelation for application!

Deuteronomy 30:11-14 tells us something that flies in the face of those who are resisting in their hearts!

> *For this commandment which I command you today* **is not too mysterious** *for you,* **nor is it far off.** *It is* **not in heaven,** *that you should say,* **'Who will** *ascend into heaven for us and* **bring it to us,** *that we may hear it and do it?' Nor is it beyond the sea, that you should say,* **'Who will go over the sea** *for us and* **bring it to us,** *that we may hear it and do it?' But* **the word is** *very* **near you,** *in your* **mouth** *and in your* **heart, that you may do it.**

At the end of the day, it's what's in our hearts that makes the Word hard or easy, simple or complicated. Our hearts make us capable of hearing, understanding, and obeying. As Isaiah taught, willingness is the precursor to obedience (Isaiah 1:19)!

In other words, there is nothing hard or mysterious about how any of this works. Make a choice for righteousness; plant the seeds of righteousness in your heart. Nurture the seed through thought, study, prayer, and meditation, and God Himself will lead you in the *"way (path) of righteousness where there is life and no death."* (Proverbs 12:28)

Remember, ears that don't want to obey don't want to hear and understand lest they be convicted by their own conscience to change, Matthew 13:15.

The *Immutable Law of the Seed* is incredibly simple. Nothing makes it hard or difficult unless we need it to be hard and confusing to provide us with an excuse for not understanding.

Divine Prescriptions

- Take time to ponder what God spoke to you in this chapter.
- Ask Him, "In light of what I'm seeing, what are you speaking to me?"
- Then, "How do I apply what I'm seeing to my life?"
- Regardless of How I personally feel about what you're showing me, "You are my Lord. I am willing to follow your leadership."
- I am willing for you to bring me to the place of trusting and applying everything you speak to me."

23. Discerning The Voice of God

Jesus' most frequent instruction is probably the most ignored!

Hearing ears can discern the difference between the voice of God speaking in our hearts and our voice speaking from our hearts (Jeremiah 23:16, Ezekiel 13:17)!

One of the great challenges concerning heart issues is the similarities between the function of the heart and the function of the mind! Honestly, I've met very few people who can tell the difference. I began pioneering this message of the heart over fifty years ago. I have seen numerous people attempt to teach about the heart with very good intentions. But in most of those situations, they confused the function of the heart and mind, or very often the heart and the brain! The first goal of Heart Physics[25] is to learn to recognize and distinguish the difference between the voice of God speaking into our hearts and our own voice!

The book of Revelation from Chapters 2:1-3:22 provides us with the most profound reason we need to be able to hear and trust the voice of God. One of the primary things we learn from these Scriptures is that while the written Word is the foundation of everything God has to say to us, <u>it is not fully</u> adequate to show us how to apply it!

25 https://heartphysics.com/

This passage in Revelation provides an appraisal of churches that actually existed at the time the Revelation was given. In fact, these verses are seven individual letters written to each of the churches and to be passed around to all the churches! In these seven letters, we can anticipate the corruption and false doctrines that will disempower the body of Christ until the rapture!

What we often fail to realize is that these seven churches provide a prophetic profile of the history of the church, beginning with the apostolic church and ending with the compromised Laodicean Church!

> **DESPITE THE THOUSANDS OF THINGS THAT CAN GO WRONG, THERE IS ONLY ONE SOLUTION!**

Each of these churches faced incredible challenges and persecution. To add to their issues, they were being infiltrated with immorality, controlling leadership, false prophets, and corrupt doctrine. When we consider that the Laodicean church represents the age in which we now live, we would do well to heed the one and only antidote to all these issues: Hear what the Spirit is saying to the churches! Despite the thousands of things that can go wrong, there is only one solution!

The Lord is our Shepherd: Jehovah-Rohi! A Shepherd's primary responsibilities are to lead, feed, and protect. If God is not doing these things, He is denying His name. The problem, however, is not that God is not leading, feeding, and protecting. The problem is the human race has become so consumed with the cares of this life or hardened by sin that we have lost our ability to hear and discern the voice of God!

God is always seeking to lead us (Psalm 23:1) in paths of righteousness where there is life and no death (Proverbs 12:28)! In other words; He is always offering leadership that is tailor-made for whatever situation we face. He doesn't leave us, fail us, or forsake us (Hebrews 13:5, Deuteronomy 31:6-8)! He never stops attempting to give us the Abundant Life. We don't earn it, but we do have to listen for His voice, search it out, and prayerfully ponder until we understand and follow!

So, we have to ask, "How did the people of Jesus' day have hearing discerning hearts?" Let's start with Jesus' express purpose, *"It has been given to you to know the mysteries of the kingdom of heaven, but to them it has not been given."* (Mark 4:11)

Both those who were followers of Christ and those "who were not" were taught in parables. The difference between the two groups was simple! One group had a heart to hear; the other didn't want to hear. One group hungered and thirsted for righteousness; the other didn't want change in their religious ideology! One group was teachable and open to instruction; the other was foolish and unteachable. … (unteachable) *"fools despise wisdom and instruction."* (Proverbs 1:7)

In order to communicate spiritual truth with those who had the heart to understand, it became impossible for those who were too carnal-minded to understand! The seed was good; it was the Word of the Kingdom. Sadly, for so many, the soil of their hearts would not receive and hold to the Words of Jesus. They all heard the same Word, but not all who heard it were willing to understand that, which would challenge their beliefs, preferences, and opinions!

The people of Jesus' day had all been taught the Word of God. But hearing the Scripture alone doesn't mean we will hear and understand. Audibly hearing or reading the Scriptures is simply the first step: knowledge! By itself, however, knowledge merely puffs up the ego but does not edify (1 Corinthians 8:1).

In what seems to be a prophetic description of Jesus' ministry, the writer warns that when the message is proclaimed that could bring the hearer to rest, it could also destroy them. Why? Because of the way they read/hear the Scriptures!

> *"This is the refreshing"; Yet they would not hear. But the word of the Lord was to them, "Precept upon precept, … Line upon line, Here a little, there a little,"* **That they might go and fall backward, and be broken And snared and caught. Therefore hear the word of the Lord.** (Isaiah 28:12-14)

Jesus revealed a simple truth that exposes a concept that is totally foreign to most of the body of Christ: *"Hearing without seeking the information without seeking God and His righteousness!"*

Jesus explained that having the Scripture without the logos leaves the reader/hearer to interpret what they hear based on their preferences. *"You search the Scriptures, for in them you think you have eternal life; and these are they which testify of Me. But you are not willing to **come to Me** that you may have life."* (John 8:39-40)

On one occasion, an expert in the law questioned Jesus. *"Teacher,"* he asked, *"what must I do to inherit eternal life?"*

Jesus answered the man's question with two questions. *"What is written in the Law?"* he replied. *"How do you read it?"* (Luke 10:25-26 NIV) Regardless of what the Scriptures say, we hear what we are listening to hear; we find what we are truly seeking!

1 Corinthians 2:9 gives us our first insight into why we are unable to discern the voice of the Lord: *"Eye has not seen, nor ear heard, nor have entered into the heart of man the things which God has prepared for those who love Him."*

God is offering mankind something beyond human comprehension. It **IS** too good to be true! It is better than anything we have seen, heard, or imagined. Consequently, we tend to attempt to reduce the promises of the Kingdom to the capacity of our finite mind rather than opening our hearts to hear that which challenges every fiber of our being.

Here's the solution, *"God has revealed them to us through His Spirit. For the Spirit searches all…, the deep things of God. …that we might know the things that have been freely given to us by God.* (1 Corinthians 2:10-15) We cannot unravel the mysteries of the Kingdom with our intellectual minds. The degree of thought, prayer, study, pondering, considering, and meditation we put into the word we hear is all about opening our hearts to hear and understand God beyond the natural limits of man!

When Paul speaks of his teaching of the Scripture, he says, *"These things we also speak, not in words which man's wisdom teaches but which the Holy Spirit teaches, **comparing spiritual things with spiritual**."* (1 Corinthians 2:13)

Over time, the Hebrews began to honor the interpretations of the Scripture provided by the "scholars" more than they valued the actual Scripture. This gave rise to the Talmud and many other writings that Jesus constantly accused them of exalting above the word of God. It was the tradition of men! They didn't honor the two most important Scriptures in the Torah: *Love God and love people* (Deuteronomy 6:5, Leviticus 19:18).

As Jesus explained, they studied for knowledge but were not looking for God or His righteousness. Their own religious concepts of righteousness were more stringent than the Bible's, but they were completely incongruent with God's expressed goals.

One of the first ways we discern the voice of God is when we compare spiritual things with spiritual things. The term "spiritual things" literally means "non-carnal." In other words, we do not go to the secular world to understand spiritual reality. We always use Scripture to interpret Scripture. Nearly everything in the New Testament can be found in the Old Testament. Likewise, there are often several verses that discuss the same subject matter. Until we compare them all, Spiritual with Spiritual, we have a very limited, one-dimensional interpretation of the Scripture. *"The natural man does not receive the things of the Spirit of God, for they are foolishness to him; nor can he know them, because they are **spiritually discerned.**"* (1 Corinthians 2:13-14)

> ONE OF THE FIRST WAYS WE DISCERN THE VOICE OF GOD IS WHEN WE COMPARE SPIRITUAL THINGS WITH SPIRITUAL THINGS.

Here, we see what most miss. Even when we diligently and thoroughly study the Scripture, we still need the Holy Spirit to serve as our teacher. We need to enlighten our hearts beyond human understanding.

The word discern can mean to distinguish, i.e., separate the parts and see all the factors. The Holy Spirit can show us multiple dimensions of a single truth. But even if we reach this point of discerning the voice of God this is where we usually "run off the tracks."

The natural mind seeks to preserve the ego, but the *heart* seeks to preserve our identity! Our ego is our false identity built on the carnal values and principles of the World System. It preserves our false sense of identity by proving that we are "right!" For the ego, being wrong is a form of death to the person we believe ourselves to be.

The Immutable Law of the Seed

Once we form an opinion or create a belief, the mind tends to look for and notice those things that will prove those opinions and beliefs to be correct. Simultaneously, it will block out input that would prove us wrong. Thus, you realize this is why the *Immutable Law of The Seed* tells us we always get more of what we've already got. Therefore, intellectually approaching the Scripture will determine "how we read it." We read it to confirm what we already believe!

This is why the Bible in the hands of a carnal person will never bring that person the Life of God! The written Word, without God's wisdom for application, becomes a false confirmation of the lies we already believe.

I love the Word of God; it is the bedrock of learning to hear God's voice. But at the end of the day, in its written form, it is still only information. Jesus taught us that we need to hear that information, understand it, and be willing to apply it. At that point, we move past mere information. There are two more elements essential to becoming overcomers when we seek to apply God's Word. We need His wisdom and His grace (power/ability capacity)!

If the written Word was adequate to provide absolute victory, Jesus would never have added this admonition to His letters to the churches: *"He who has an ear, let him hear what the Spirit says to the churches."* (Revelation 3:12)

Remember, Israel had the Scripture for centuries, but it wasn't until Jesus came that they could perceive God's motives and intentions! God's motive was to make us one with Him, and His motive was love!

Even though we know that… we still read His Words without factoring in those same motives and intentions. Therefore, we read and interpret based on our motives and intentions, which are too often subconsciously motivated to confirm our thoughts and opinions.

The ultimate exercise in comparing Spiritual things to Spiritual things is to go to the only model we have of a Spiritual life: Jesus!

We will never get our doctrine straight, and we'll never find meaningful application of the word until we look at it through Jesus' life, ministry, teaching, death, burial, and resurrection! Rather than our primary study being the pursuit of perfect doctrine, we should look at Jesus to see a perfect life. It should be our goal to be like Him in every way! He brings the word to life in ways that are beyond words.

In this book, I have provided thought-provoking questions at the end of each chapter that will help you open your heart to the Great teacher as you develop a heart that discerns and understands!

Divine Prescriptions

- Take time to ponder what God spoke to you in this chapter.
- Ask Him, "In light of what I'm seeing, what are you speaking to me?"
- Then, "How do I apply what I'm seeing to my life?"
- Regardless of How I personally feel about what you're showing me, "You are my Lord. I am willing to follow your leadership."
- I am willing for you to bring me to the place of trusting and applying everything you speak to me."

24. A Teachable Heart

The only people who can't be helped are the unteachable!

In a previous chapter, we pointed out that repentance is the starting point for having a heart that can receive the Word of the Kingdom of Heaven. Sadly, humanistic Christianity wants everything to be peppy, positive, and totally non-threatening! In many churches, it is unpopular to deal with sin, repentance, or anything that places responsibility on the believer.

As previously discussed, repentance isn't merely about dealing with sinful behavior. Repentance has an incredibly important, positive function in the process of transformation!

Repentance is one of the three main aspects of transformation: put off the old man, renew the mind, and put on the new man! Repentance involves renewing the mind and surrendering our thoughts and opinions to God's truth!

Both John the Baptist and Jesus presented repentance as the first step in a journey toward The Kingdom of Heaven. The Jews, to whom they were speaking, already had somewhat of a grasp on the Kingdom of God. They understood the need to surrender to God. Sadly, their view of God was so negative and legalistic that they had no concept of entering the

Kingdom of Heaven, i.e., the realm where we have access to the resources of Heaven!

Upon Jesus' arrival, they were about to hear and see the Messiah represent God in all His goodness, the way He really is. This would stand in sharp contrast to everything they had been taught by the religious establishment! However, if they didn't have a repentant, teachable attitude, they would never receive His revelation of God!

In his book, *Hebrew Word Pictures*,[26] Dr. Frank Seekins says this about the word repentance: It was a word that originally had to do with being taken captive. The captors would force their hostages to watch their houses, crops, and all they owned being burned. By doing this, they knew they had nothing to return to. This concept renders the interpretation: Destroy the house, leave nothing behind!

The Israelites who came out of Egypt, frequently wanted to return to Egypt, i.e., the land of captivity. They even considered forcibly overthrowing Moses' leadership so they could return to their slavery. Hebrews 11:13-15 shines light on what we can learn from them. In this passage, the writer of Hebrews explains the attitude of the patriarchs that followed God:

> *They were strangers and pilgrims on the earth. For they that say such things declare plainly that they seek a country (kingdom). And truly, if they had been mindful of that country from whence they came out, they might have had opportunity to have returned.* (KJV)

> **REPENTANCE IS ABOUT RETHINKING OUR DECISIONS AND DECIDING WHETHER TO FOLLOW OUR WILL OR GOD'S WILL.**

Repentance is not about shame and guilt. It is about rethinking our decisions and deciding whether to follow our will or God's will. This brings us to the ultimate Hebrew meaning of repentance: burn the house down and burn all the bridges, so there is nothing to return to and no way to get there.

---

26   Hebrew Word Pictures, Dr. Frank T. Seekins, copyright 2020

The word "repent" includes the Hebrew letter Bet, which can refer to either the heart or a house. This implies that we are leaving one house/country/kingdom in pursuit of another. If the kingdom we left behind still exists, it could be a constant tug on our hearts! The way to escape that continual temptation is to burn all your bridges and burn down that life completely. When there is nothing to return to, there is no temptation!

Dr Seekins continues to explain: "Once we have destroyed the home of captivity, we are ready to enter our real home, which is designed for who we really are! In that home, we are safe, loved, and whole. This is where we find unconditional and relational love, peace, and acceptance (Ephesians 1:6)."

Over the years, I have learned to recognize those who will backslide unless they get the help they need. People who often talk about their old life, especially when they talk about how good it was, are those who will return to that life of captivity. By thinking back on their past with joy, they are actually meditating on that life and the pleasures of sin, thereby planting seeds in their hearts that produce bad fruit, unto unrighteousness!

When I gave my life to the Lord, I had no religious teaching at all. I had never heard the word "repentance." But I could hear the voice of God in my heart. I went home and flushed about $1000 in drugs down the toilet. I quit the band I was in. I didn't want to be in that wicked environment. I distanced myself from people who attempted to influence me to do drugs and party with them.

I didn't do any of those things because I thought I had to. I didn't want anything that would draw me back into that life. Void of biblical wisdom, I followed the voice of God in my heart into one of the "First Truths" of entering the Kingdom of Heaven. I burned down everything that connected me to the life that had held me captive for so many years. However, I was never unkind or judgmental to the people "from that world." By showing them the love of God and living my life before them, I eventually led many of those friends to Jesus.

The repentant heart is teachable, adaptable, and willing to hear and follow God, whether it is in the written Word or the Word He speaks in their hearts. The heart of repentance is the embodiment of humility!

Romans 12:16 offers one of the most profound, useful, yet overlooked pieces of scriptural wisdom. This Scripture addresses the root of almost all of our struggles. *"Do not be wise in your own opinion."* Those who are wise in their own opinion are not open to the input of those who are more experienced, and they're not actually open to God's leadership!

God has a view and opinion, and according to the original language, His view and opinion are the reality. We have views and opinions, but unfortunately, our views and opinions rarely align with His. We have an imaginary sense of reality based on our intellectual assessments. This is the primary reason believers cannot hear the voice of God in their hearts. We so completely trust our opinions, that we think they represent reality.

God can only lead the humble. Please realize that I am not talking about false religious humility. Religion would have us believe that humility is to hang your head and feel like you're nothing! That is actually a form of pride and arrogance.

Remember, sin is not just when someone commits an obviously wicked or heinous act. According to Romans 3:23, sin is anything that causes us to fall short of the glory of God! In the Greek, the words "fall short" mean to be inferior.

The glory of God is when God manifests Himself in a way that makes it possible for people to see Him as He is. God's glory was first manifested in creation. However, since we have accepted the views and opinions of those who promote false science, we have blinded ourselves. We no longer see the glory of God in the natural world, even though it is prevalent everywhere we look.

We rarely come up with an unscriptural opinion on our own. According to Jesus, the tares, who are sons of the devil, sow these lies in the world. We learn them through family, education, government, false science, and religious influences. Regardless of where they originated or how reliable we consider the sources, these opinions that we trust more than the Word of God cause us to see and experience ourselves as inferior to who God has made us to be. What's worse is we see God as inferior to who He has declared Himself to be. This is when we must choose humility over pride, willingness over resistance, and openness over stubbornness!

1 Peter 5:5 says this, *"Likewise, you younger people, submit yourselves to your elders. Yes, all of you be submissive to one another, and be clothed with humility..."*

Contrary to the position of religious controllers, submission is not blind, mindless obedience. The civil authorities ordered Peter and John to stop preaching in the name of Jesus. The Scripture tells us to submit to civil authorities. But they didn't stop preaching. When the person in power tells us anything that is not in harmony with God's word, we are to respectfully disobey.

Submission is more about yielding and being willing to hear and consider than blind obedience. In the infamous interpretation of Ephesians 22, we are told that *"wives should submit to their husbands."* Religion has twisted this into a domination of a husband over his wife that violates Jesus' teaching. The irony is that in the previous verse, it says we should *"submit to one another."*

> **SUBMISSION IS MORE ABOUT YIELDING AND BEING WILLING TO HEAR AND CONSIDER THAN BLIND OBEDIENCE.**

So, which one is it? If we're both submitting to one another, who's going to be in charge? Neither is in charge because this is not about obedience; it's about being open and willing to consider one another. The whole point of husbands and wives submitting to one another is so they both can search the word of God and then, out of love and respect, reach a joint decision, not based on our opinions but on God's opinions.

Peter opens this passage with the admonition to submit to one another. Why? How we treat one another is a true reflection of how we relate to God. This is fruit we can examine and discover how we really relate to God! But we must understand if I am not open and willing to hear the people I can see, I am fooling myself into thinking I am open and willing to hear God when it conflicts with my opinion.

Developing a teachable heart is not nearly as complicated as we would think. Like all things, it begins with a decision. I choose to consider input from others. I am willing to always put God's word ahead of my opinions. Begin to do *HeartWork*[27] to persuade your heart of your choice. Then, observe the fruit. As I open to the people I can see, I can be assured that I am becoming more open and teachable to God!

Divine Prescriptions

- Take time to ponder what God spoke to you in this chapter.
- Ask Him, "In light of what I'm seeing, what are you speaking to me?"
- Then, "How do I apply what I'm seeing to my life?"
- Regardless of How I personally feel about what you're showing me, "You are my Lord. I am willing to follow your leadership."
- I am willing for you to bring me to the place of trusting and applying everything you speak to me."

---

[27] https://heartphysics.com/

25. Opening Your Understanding

Willingness to be taught opens the door to understanding!

Understanding starts with a decision, which is then cultivated by our approach to the information. But we must begin with a passion to understand! Proverbs 2:3-5 says it like this, *"If you cry out for discernment, And lift up your voice for understanding, If you seek her as silver, And search for her as for hidden treasures; Then you will understand...."*

This is more than a casual interest. This is something that occurs when we believe God's words to be the words of life. Verse five actually continues as follows: *"Then you will understand the fear of the Lord, and find the knowledge of God."*

This word for fear is not the dread of God hurting you. It is the awe and reverence of God that bring us to love and worship!

When we love God and are in awe of Him, our greatest concern is anything that would damage our relationship with Him. When our relationship is more important than theological pursuits, proving ourselves right, or any other carnal motivation, when our relationship is the most important thing, it changes everything about our passion to nurture the seed that has been sown in our hearts. When we understand and value the fear of the Lord (our most important relationship), the eyes of our hearts open, and we can see God at work in our situation.

> TOO OFTEN, WE ATTEMPT TO UNDERSTAND GOD'S WORK IN A SITUATION BASED ON OUR PREVIOUSLY HELD DOCTRINES OR RELIGIOUS THOUGHTS.

Too often, we attempt to understand God's work in a situation based on our previously held doctrines or religious thoughts. This approach leads to presumption and judgment against God, which makes it impossible to perceive what God is actually doing. When everything is based on "relationship first," our motivation and perception change.

Few believers understand the "fear of the Lord" because they aren't seeking it. They believe it is something negative to be dreaded. But for those who desire a meaningful relationship with God, it doesn't matter if they do or do not know the interpretation. They intuitively put the relationship first, and all else falls into place.

The Hebrew word for knowledge is "yada." A deep dive into the meaning of this word takes us far beyond knowledge as mere information.

The first letter in "yada" is "Yud." This represents a message directly from God that reveals God's hand, i.e., God's working/ways as it applies to the word/seed we seek to plant in our hearts!

The second letter in "yada" is the Dalet. The "dalet" represents a door that opens to a new path. Since there is a new path, we must be willing to walk that path, even when we don't fully realize where it leads. Those who don't want to walk a new path get stuck at this point. They don't want to change. They want to walk the path they have always walked!

The last letter in "yada" is Ayin. This letter represents perception, i.e., spiritual sight. It gives us the ability to see beyond the natural realm and into other dimensions that go far beyond the natural mind! It gives us a perception of the future and how our actions could have long-term consequences. All of these factors combined represent discernment.

Opening Your Understanding

Discernment allows us to perceive all the individual pieces. This is the key to understanding. Once we perceive all the pieces, understanding brings them together in ways that make us realize that all the pieces form a whole! But it doesn't stop there. Once we understand the fear of the Lord, our hearts open to wisdom.

The last verse takes us to the ultimate goal: application. Verse 7 tells us that when we are motivated by the fear of the Lord, we grasp the working of God. But He doesn't leave us with mere information. *"He stores up sound wisdom for the upright."*

Wisdom has a very broad meaning. However, it is always about practical application. It is one thing to know what needs to be done; it is an entirely different thing to know how to do it!

The Hebrew word for wisdom is "chakam." The root word is spelled Chet – Kaf – Mem. Chet represents a new beginning where God and man are in harmony. This letter refers to the power of choice. Chet allows us to enter into infinite possibilities while enjoying the protection of God.

The Kaf represents an empty container waiting and longing to be filled with God's presence and wisdom. The Kaf gives form. This means that which we only know by faith can take form in this physical world. It is the manifestation of that which is believed!

The final letter is the Mem, which, as used in this word, is called a closed Mem. This represents God's private knowledge/instruction. This is when God leads you by the Holy Spirit to understand how to apply the Word you're hearing in your current situation. It is a tailor-made plan for you!

This could read something like this: As our heart cries out to be in perfect oneness with the Father, we harmonize with God and experience a new beginning. As we wait to be filled with God's presence, we listen to receive God's personal leadership for application and protection, which ensures absolute success!

Understanding is a gift from God, but it does not come automatically; it must be sought with all our hearts! It is this hunger that opens our hearts to knowledge, understanding, and wisdom!

The Immutable Law of the Seed

Divine Prescription

- Take time to ponder what God spoke to you in this chapter.
- Ask Him, "In light of what I'm seeing, what are you speaking to me?"
- Then, "How do I apply what I'm seeing to my life?"
- Regardless of How I personally feel about what you're showing me, "You are my Lord. I am willing to follow your leadership."
- I am willing for you to bring me to the place of trusting and applying everything you speak to me."

26. Activating The Seed

Faith that is not activated never nurtures the seed and never produces fruit!

In Chapter 19, we discussed the concept of "the measure you meet." We understand this to be a reference to the concept that what you put into the Word of the Kingdom that you hear will determine the fruit that comes back from that seed.

I find it interesting that Jesus didn't explain what this looks like when put into practice. He had no need to do that; they knew the Scriptures, so they knew the many ways the Bible taught them to nurture their hearts and cause the seed to grow. Their problem, however, was the fact that even though this had been in the Scripture, all the way back to Moses, the legalistic, religious leaders never taught it.

Please keep in mind that I'm not talking about dead works, where you think that doing biblically-based *HeartWork* will move God for you. Nurturing the seed and the soil is something we do, not to affect God but to affect our own hearts.

Meditation is taught all through the Scriptures. But it doesn't always use the word "meditate." Meditation, like prayer, can be done in many ways. But there are key elements that will always be present in any form of biblical meditation we pursue! Since much of this has been adequately discussed in previous chapters, we will not repeat it here.

In Joel 3, the prophet warns of an impending war. The instructions he gave were a combination of practical preparation and preparing their hearts. He said, *"Beat your plowshares into swords And your pruning hooks into spears; Let the weak say, 'I am strong.'"* (Joel 3:9-10)

When he said Let the weak say they are strong, this can bring up negative memories of a very shallow teaching about "confessing the Word," which was very prominent from the 1970s through the 1990s and is still promoted by various groups. They earned the description of "Name it and claim it." Like so many doctrines that have emerged over the years, it wasn't bad doctrine, but it was incomplete; it left out the heart!

The word "say" in this passage of Scripture is the same Hebrew word that was used in Genesis of God when He spoke creation into existence. There is more than one Hebrew word translated as "say or said." One of those words places all the emphasis on the act of speaking words. But the Hebrew word used of God in creation is the same word used here where we are told to "confess" that we are strong, even though in our natural abilities we know that we are weak.

> **HE OPERATED IN THE IMMUTABLE LAW OF THE SEED IN ORDER TO CREATE ALL THINGS THAT EXIST.**

The Hebrew word translated as say, is "Amar." It can also mean "to see and say!" Many scholars point out that this word implies that God spoke with intention, and before He spoke, He conceived the outcome in His heart. He didn't casually speak words. The Words He spoke were the seeds that would be planted in the soil of the universe that would produce a continual harvest. In other words, He operated in the *Immutable Law of the Seed* in order to create all things that exist. He is our model for faith.

That this word can be interpreted as "say and see" tells us that He saw the *end from the beginning* in His heart. His intention was that His words would produce the outcome that He saw in His heart. This is the exact process that Jesus described when teaching about faith in Mark 11:22-

24. In creation, God modeled faith. He created the *Immutable Law of the Seed*, to be the primary law of all creation. This law supersedes all the laws of physics. This concept is predominant in the New Testament.

All the times Jesus healed the sick or worked a miracle, He seemed to violate the known laws of physics. However, He didn't violate them; He merely employed a higher law of physics. The Immutable Law of the Seed is one of the highest laws of physics, and God deliberately programmed this into creation. It is the easiest law to understand and apply, yet because of the influences of religion, it has been totally ignored!

The *Law of the Seed* is utilized to activate faith, although this phrase is never used in English! Read Philemon 1:6, *"That the communication of thy faith may become effectual by the acknowledging of every good thing which is in you in Christ Jesus."* (KJV)

The following is a breakdown of nearly every word in that passage.

- **Communication:** Koinonia, i.e., What we share with Christ

- **Effectual:** effective, activated, energized, capable of doing, i.e., workable, powerful

- **Acknowledging:** epi-gnosis, recognizing, experiential knowledge,
    - It is more intense than gnosis, having knowledge, because it expresses a more thorough participation in the acquiring of knowledge on the part of the learner.

- **Every:** all forms, i.e., everything

- **Good:** useful, pleasing, desirable, harmonious

- **In You:** because He is in you by the Holy Spirit, all of His attributes are in you. You have the latent life of Christ and all He is in you now, although they may not be activated by your faith!

- **In Christ:** Christ in you is the power of the resurrection life. Christ in you affects your character and the way you interact with the world around you.
    - You, in Christ, affect the way you interact with God.

Religion would have us believe that we solve our problems and become better "Christians" if we continually acknowledge all the bad things in our lives. As logical as this sounds, it contradicts Jesus' teaching. Constantly reminding ourselves of all that is wrong about us is to actively plant thorns in the garden of our hearts, which chokes out the seed/Word of the Kingdom!

In 1 John 1:9, we are told to confess our sins.... The word confess is a compound word meaning say the same thing and logos. This goes much further than merely admitting to all our failures. It is absolutely essential that we own and acknowledge our sins with no excuses and no one to blame. But it is equally essential that we acknowledge what the logos says about our sins. They are forgiven; we are loved and accepted; we have been made righteous in Christ, and much more. There is far more to acknowledge what Jesus did for our sins than there is about our failures!

The apostle Paul explains that if we want to share/koinonia in all that Christ is, we have to **acknowledge every good thing that is in us** as a result of being in Him. This is actively and deliberately planting and nurturing the Word/seed of the Kingdom in our hearts while activating our faith/trust in God's Immutable Law of the Seed!

One of the most powerful *HeartWork* tools I have developed is the *Prayer Organizer*.[28] This was developed for use in my personal life. Using the *Prayer Organizer* established my Heart in my identity in Christ more than any tool I have ever developed. Consequently, I was able to walk out of a lifelong disease, recover from incredible debt due to medical bills, and navigate my way to my ultimate destiny!

I recommend using the *Prayer Organizer* daily until you have no capacity to see yourself in any way other than who you are in Christ! Even if you don't follow the entire process every day, be sure to use the section on the names of God daily! Be sure to read and follow the instructions so you will have the optimal impact on your heart!

- Look at all the names of God and those attributes that relate to that name.
- Pay close attention to see how Jesus has fulfilled (brought to the fullness) the attributes of God's names.

---

[28] https://impactministries.com/product/the-prayer-organizer/

- Then, write, in your own words, the attributes that you choose to activate.
- Transpose that list into a statement that is:
  - Personal: I, not we
  - Positive: never focus on what you're attempting to overcome; focus on and acknowledge what is already yours in Christ.
  - Present tense: Never state it as something you hope for but something you already have because you are in Christ!

If you want more thorough instructions, get my book Heaven on Earth. It goes into great detail about Jesus' prayer life and what He taught about prayer!

Divine Prescription

- Take time to ponder what God spoke to you in this chapter.
- Ask Him, "In light of what I'm seeing, what are you speaking to me?"
- Then, "How do I apply what I'm seeing to my life?"
- Regardless of How I personally feel about what you're showing me, "You are my Lord. I am willing to follow your leadership."
- I am willing for you to bring me to the place of trusting and applying everything you speak to me."

27. Watching Over The Seed

The price of freedom is eternal vigilance![29]

Truer words have never been spoken! This quote applies to civil liberties and freedom from governmental oppression, but possibly even more important is its significance in relation to the *Immutable Law of the Seed*!

As humans, we tend to search for instant gratification and "easy fixes." Even when we take steps to free ourselves from oppression, we tend to stop doing what works the moment we get relief from our pain. Then, when we slip back into our problems, we get what I call "spiritual amnesia." We seem to think that what we are doing has never worked, so we jump to something else!

When we consider the metaphor of our heart being a garden, wherein we plant the seeds of the Kingdom, we must realize that raising a crop is unending. Just like the weeds that seem to mysteriously appear in our gardens, thorns begin to grow in our hearts. This is the result of being in a world that is inundated with the sin principle. Faced with this constant presence of evil, we can never allow ourselves to become complacent about guarding our hearts!

---
29   Quote often attributed to Thomas Jefferson but used by others, including John Philpot Curran, Tom Paine, Wendell Phillips, and Abraham Lincoln

The weeds never stop growing, and the birds continuously drop all kinds of seeds that rob the soil of nutrients. Therefore, it has to be continuously watered, fertilized, and weeded! This is why we must be endlessly vigilant to guard and nurture our hearts and the seeds we've planted.

Nearly every believer is familiar with Proverbs 4:23, *"Keep your heart with all diligence, For out of it spring the issues of life."* The Amplified Bible says it like this. *"Keep and guard your heart with all vigilance and above all that you guard."* (AMP)

As both of these translations point out, everything about the quality of our lives flows from our hearts, where the seed is planted. This verse explicitly warns of the dire consequences if we fail to guard our hearts, which is rarely understood in 21st-century Christianity! I have met few believers who have any clue as to how and why they need to vigilantly guard their hearts.

In this verse in Proverbs, as well as dozens of others, we are told to *"keep"* our hearts, or *"keep"* God's Word. The Hebrew word for "keep" is an interesting word: natsar! The Greek counterpart in the New Testament is very similar; it means to guard, watch over, and keep an eye on it, maintain things entrusted to us, and especially keep the truths of God. (The Word of the Kingdom).

Unfortunately, "keep" is usually interpreted to mean strict obedience. But it actually has more to do with our attitude than our behavior. (The right attitude always leads to the correct behavior, but the proper behavior can be poisoned by a bad attitude!) The Hebrew word for "keep" lends itself to the idea of holding something dear, watching over it, or considering it precious. Proverbs 4:23 presents the idea of continual attentive watchfulness, i.e., vigilance!

Normally, when we mention stewardship, people's thoughts go immediately to money. The truth is that stewardship is about our management of all the resources available to us. However, the most precious resource we are to keep, watch over, and treat as precious is our own heart!

Why is this so important? If we fail to tend to the soil of our hearts, our entire lives can change course, and we won't understand what's happening or why it's happening!

Watching Over The Seed

There are three factors that determine how much fruit a seed bears: the quality of the seed, the condition of the soil, and the way we care for the soil after the seed has been planted. All of these fall under the purview of guarding, i.e., keeping and nurturing our hearts.

To better understand this awesome responsibility, let's take a closer look at the meanings of the Hebrew letters. The root of "natsar" is spelled Nun – Tsade – Resh. These letters present a fuller concept of the Word "keep."

"Nun" represents humility, depicted in the fact that both ends of the letter are bent over in humility. This can symbolize bowing down while reaching up to God. "Nun" also represents a fish. Fish are flexible and adaptable; they navigate through the water around rocks and debris, all while negotiating the currents. One of the most exciting aspects of Nun is that it also represents a faith that isn't immediately seen but emerges in a time of need.

The "Tsade" represents the righteous person and the righteousness of the Creator. It strives to be true and loving while upholding justice and fairness. The Tsade is straight, not crooked. There is nothing hidden. There are no unseen traps in the path of righteousness. Besides being honest with others, the Tsade is fully honest with its own conscience.

> THE "TSADE" REPRESENTS THE RIGHTEOUS PERSON AND THE RIGHTEOUSNESS OF THE CREATOR.

The "Tsade" is a picture of a fish hook pulling toward something inescapable. The fish seems to be caught by the hook and drawn to God's righteousness.

Finally, and most importantly, righteousness and humility are the two defining traits of the Tsade.

The final letter is "Resh. The ancient Picture of the resh represents a head, or as in the head of something. It conveys the idea of the highest importance. One source says the Resh represents the choice between greatness and degradation. Finally, the Resh points toward repentance, i.e., a humble teachable attitude.

Based on the meanings of the word "keep," how do we functionally keep or guard our hearts? The Old Testament priests wore a breastplate that covered their hearts, depicting a guard or protection for the heart. In Ephesians 6:14, Paul refers to it as the breastplate of righteousness. Righteousness is what guards the heart. I'm not talking about legalistic or positional righteousness that is given to all believers in Christ as a free gift. I'm referring to our commitment to humble ourselves and yield to the Holy Spirit as He leads us in paths of righteousness (Psalm 23:3).

Based on the meanings of the letters, this would imply that righteousness is the highest and most important factor we must cling to when guarding our hearts.

A pocket in the priest's breastplate held the Urim and Thummim. As far as we know, the Urim and Thummim were simply two different colored stones. One meant yes, and the other meant no!

When Israel needed to go to war or make other important decisions, but no one had heard from God through prophecy or dreams, they would go to the priest who would prayerfully utilize the Urim and Thummim.

He would state a possible course of action and prayerfully reach inside the breastplate's pocket to withdraw one of the stones. One color of stone meant yes, and the other meant no! Israel won some very decisive battles and developed military strategies utilizing the Urim and Thummim!

Among the many types that emerge from the breastplate and the Urim and Thummim, the most significant is this: The heart that is committed to following God's righteousness can always recognize the appropriate choice through the leadership of the Holy Spirit... who always leads us in the path of righteousness!

> **THE BIBLE TELLS US ALWAYS TO HAVE TWO OR THREE WITNESSES WHEN SEARCHING FOR THE TRUTH.**

The Bible tells us always to have two or three witnesses when searching for the truth. I'm not talking about a subjective, mystical feeling that guides us. God has provided us with three reliable witnesses who are always present, ready, willing, and able to provide leadership that is more accurate and dependable than anything the human mind can conceive: the Scripture, the Spirit, and our conscience. When those three are in harmony, we can always make a decision that will guard and guide our hearts while facilitating the growth of the seed!

This simple word "keep" creates the picture of a humble and teachable person. They hunger and thirst for the righteousness that is found in Christ. When the Word of the Kingdom is scattered/preached by a Sower, the humble pay attention. Like the "Nun," which represents the fish navigating the flow of the water and the obstacles, the humble remains forever teachable, flexible, and adaptable!

The humility and hunger for righteousness that embodies the person who "keeps" his or her heart is someone God can raise up and strengthen by grace.

> *Be clothed with humility, for 'God **resists** the proud, But gives grace to the humble.' Therefore humble yourselves under the mighty hand of God that He may exalt you in **due time**.* (1 Peter 5:5-6)

The word "resist" means to stand in opposition. When a person is proud, they are yielding to the same inherent, unteachable attitude that drove Lucifer to rebel (1 Timothy 3:6). The unteachable is not only foolish but trapped in pride. In their arrogance, they exalt their opinion above God's opinion. Consequently, their sense of reality is corrupted. This perversion of reality ensures that all their choices lead to destructive consequences.

Based on this Scripture, the seed always produces its precious fruit in due time. When is the elusive "due time" to which Peter refers? Is this a reference to some mystical timing of God that will happen as the result of His arbitrary timing? No! The Book of Galatians makes this much clearer.

Everything that occurs in a garden is based on the seasons. There is a season to sow, a season to reap, and a season to gather a harvest (Ecclesiastes 3:1). We can understand that the seasons are environmental conditions that support everything from sowing the seed to reaping the harvest! Producing a crop is not nearly as mystical as it often seems. God is not waiting for some unique, unexplainable moment to allow the fruit to grow. It comes in the appropriate season! Listen to this scripture:

The Immutable Law of the Seed

*He who sows to his flesh will of the flesh reap corruption, but he who sows to the Spirit will of the Spirit reap everlasting life (zoe). And let us not grow weary while doing good, for in **due season** we shall reap if we do not lose heart.* (Galatians 6:8-9)

In the parable of the Sower, there was one person who received the word with joy and endured **for a while.** This person became anxious and impulsive. While he is facing some tribulation and persecution, his main issue is that he stumbles because he has no "root" in him. This could be interpreted to mean He has no hold,[30] which implies that he was not established in his faith. He did not diligently watch over and keep the Word that was planted in him, i.e., he was not diligent in weeding out the thorns and nurturing the soil!

We can only exercise faith for that which we know. He may have had some religious concept of what needed to be done to make the seed produce fruit. Instead of patiently waiting for the time of harvest, he may have tried every religious formula he knew to make the fruit grow. He didn't know that all he had to do was don't grow weary and don't lose heart. The fruit will come forth in the right season.

It may surprise you to realize that we create the season for the harvest. As we nurture the seed and persuade our hearts, we create the environment that allows the seed to grow and ultimately bear fruit.

The more diligently we watch over, guard, and nurture the Word sown in our hearts, the quicker we enter into the season that bears fruit!

Your Divine Prescription is different for this chapter. I want you to ponder how to continue to keep, guard, and nurture the soil of our hearts. Pay close attention to the points that resonate with you!

Discover Your Divine Prescription

- Keep the soil nurtured and loose, just like you would in a garden, by dealing with every attitude of resistance, i.e., hardening of the soil/heart.

---

30   The Complete Word Study Dictionary: New Testament © 1992 by AMG International, Inc. Revised Edition, 1993

- Continue planting good seeds in your heart that support the healthy seed you have already planted.
  - Don't put anyone's ideas, philosophies, or doctrine ahead of what you see and read in the Bible for yourself.
  - Don't exalt anything in the Bible above Jesus' teaching, life, death, burial, and resurrection.
- Be careful who you listen to and what you listen to.
  - If it causes you to doubt or question God's Word, stay away!
  - Don't plant thorns; they will choke out the Word of the Kingdom
  - Don't let your heart get hard or indifferent.
  - Don't become wrapped up in the World's system of values, ethics, and morality.
  - Guard your heart by dealing with every thought, imagination, and temptation as they occur. Cast down anything that is contrary to the promises of God.
- Never stop nurturing the seed.
  - Ponder, meditate, quote, and talk about the Scriptures that remind you of the promise.
- Learn everything you can about what happened on the Cross, in the grave, and through the resurrection.
  - I have an audio series and a soon-to-be-released book, *Three Days That Changed the World*.[31] This takes you into the details of the Cross, the grave, and the resurrection.
  - Put on the new man – put off the old man.
- Learn to pray as Jesus prayed.
  - You may want to read my book, *Keys of the Kingdom*.[32]

---

[31] https://impactministries.com/product/three-days-that-changed-the-world/
[32] https://www.truepotentialmedia.com/product/keys-of-the-kingdom/

28. Finding The Treasure

The Immutable Law of the Seed gives us access to one of the greatest treasures in the Bible!

In Matthew 13, Jesus presented seven parables that enlightened us about many aspects of the *Immutable Law of the Seed*. One of the most enlightening may be the hidden treasure.

The treasure we are encouraged to seek is the Kingdom of Heaven. The majority of commentaries and Bible teachers believe that the Kingdom of Heaven and the Kingdom of God are the same thing. Sadly, they minimize the concept to such a state that it is robbed of its ability to motivate us to surrender all and seek the treasure.

Most Bible teachers agree that these two synonyms refer to going to heaven when we die! Heaven after death does hold a degree of compelling motivation. "Pie in the sky, in the great by-and-by" is hardly enough motivation to overcome the daily temptations of the flesh, which constantly cries out for fulfillment—now!

The significance and value of the treasure are designed to draw us to God. In fact, when we want the treasure badly enough, we become repentant and open our hearts to understanding from God's point of view.

Understanding what motivates people helps us understand the dynamic of the treasure, and it makes us effective ministers. When ministering to someone, if we don't understand their motivational preference, we may do everything we think would draw them to God only to drive them away.

Some people are moved by what is called "toward" motivation, while others are inspired by "away" motivation. Toward motivation occurs when someone is drawn toward something, while away motivation occurs when someone is compelled to move away from or avoid something.

This fits very closely with the concept of pain and pleasure motivation. Many people are motivated to take action when they either experience pain or face the expectation of pain. Others are motivated by pleasure. They are motivated to take action when they experience pleasure or have an expectation of pleasure! Based on their expectation of pain or pleasure, they are motivated to take action toward something or away from it.

> WE MUST REMEMBER THAT PAIN OR PLEASURE MAY NOT BE REAL; IT IS OFTEN AN EXPECTATION OF PAIN OR PLEASURE BASED ON CURRENTLY HELD BELIEFS.

We must remember that pain or pleasure may not be real; it is often an expectation of pain or pleasure based on currently held beliefs. Each of these different types of motivation represents what the person values: do they value the hope of pleasure or the avoidance of pain?

The Greek word agape, translated as love, literally means value. This helps us understand why the Apostle John said if you have love (value) for the world, the love (value) for the Father is not in you (1 John 2:15). When we value what the world has to offer more than we value what God has to offer we will never seek the Kingdom first. We will always seek the world, its philosophies, and provisions first!

People usually develop their value of pain and pleasure based on their upbringing, i.e., the type of motivation used by their parents. Negative parents who employ the threat of punishment to control their children tend to develop children who dread pain. They have a constant expectation of pain. The problem with this "away from" motivation is that when the threat is gone, they are no longer motivated.

Parents who offer rewards for accomplishments develop an attitude of meritocracy in their children.[33] These children are highly motivated by the expectation of reward/pleasure for their efforts.

Both of these approaches to motivation have merit and drawbacks. In ministry, both of these motivational concepts must be employed. In every situation, we have freedom of choice. The choice is always between blessing and cursing, i.e., pain and pleasure! Many liberal ministers are convinced that only positive motivation should be employed when attempting to lead people into making godly decisions. If, however, that were the case, I don't think God would have put warnings in the Scripture.

On the other hand, those who tend to be prone to legalism almost exclusively use fear and negativity to motivate believers to live a godly life.

In the parables of the Seed, there are warnings for those who will not plant and nurture the seed in their hearts. But there are also wonderful promises of rewards for those who do!

Proverbs 16:6 says, *"By mercy and truth iniquity is purged: and by the fear of the LORD men depart from evil."*

While this passage provides many insights, one thing stands out to me: Fear will affect behavior. The fear of punishment may cause many to depart from evil behavior. In this Scripture, the Hebrew "Kaphar" is translated as purge. This is not referencing a healthy concept of cleansing. 'Kaphar' is usually translated as covering. It seems this verse is saying that fear, without the presence of mercy and truth, simply leads to covering sin rather than confessing and forsaking it (Proverbs 28:13). This seems to be one of many places that points out the need for both warnings and promises.

Positive motivation seems to have a desired influence on the heart's beliefs, while negative motivation has more of an influence on behavior!

33   From Ancient Greek κράτος *kratos* 'strength, power') is the notion of a political system in which economic goods or political power are vested in individual people based on ability and talent, rather than wealth, social class, or race. Advancement in such a system is based on performance.

It is healthy and more influential when we are motivated by both the warnings and the rewards. Hebrews 11:6 says, *"...he who comes to God must believe that He is, and that He is a **rewarder** of those who diligently seek Him."*

It seems that God uses warnings to get us to stop and consider, but He uses promises to inspire and motivate us to go forward! After all, it is the **goodness of God** *that draws us to repentance* (Romans 2:4). While it doesn't seem that fear effectively draws us to repentance, it may make us stop and reconsider our direction.

When we realize the benefits that are ours by surrendering our lives to God, juxtaposed against the consequences of continuing to resist, we will gladly do it. But warnings without promises do not move people to true repentance. Therefore, we must have some degree of comprehension of the treasure before we will be motivated to seek it!

> **WHEN WE VALUE SOMETHING, WE TEND TO DESIRE IT.**

When we value something, we tend to desire it. When desire reaches a strong enough drive, we will seek the things of God. When we seek, He will always reveal them to us (1 Corinthians 2:10, Matthew 7:7).

So then, the question begging to be answered is this: What is the treasure? This is it: *"It has been given to you to know **the mysteries of the kingdom of heaven.**"* (Matthew 13:1) Please remember the word translated as "know" is experiential knowledge. Jesus told us that when we surrender to His Lordship, we are given everlasting life! In Greek, the word is Zoe. Zoe is not merely how long we live; it is about the quality of the life we live. One of the best Greek language resources[34] says "zoe" is the quality of life possessed by the one who gives it![35]

The Kingdom of Heaven is a realm we enter to experience this quality of Jesus possessed. This is where we have access to all the resources of Heaven! Everything Jesus taught and modeled showed us the way to enter the Kingdom of God **and** the Kingdom of Heaven. As previously explained,

---

[34] Biblico-Theological Lexicon of New testament Greek, Hermann Cremer ,Edinburgh: T&T Clark, p 270,274, 721
[35] Thayer's Greek Lexicon, PC Study Bible formatted Electronic Database. Copyright © 2006 by Biblesoft, Inc. All rights reserved.

the Kingdom of God is entering into the dominion of Lordship. This is the precursor to the Kingdom of Heaven.

Religion has made the Kingdom of Heaven a reference to what we experience after we die. Quality of life after we die is a motivator, but most people are far more motivated by what will bring them quality of life in the "here and now!" The Kingdom of Heaven is tantamount to living in heaven before you die!

Jesus presented six supplemental parables about the seed and the Kingdom of Heaven that give us a little more insight into attaining the treasure. Remember, we attain the treasure when we are open and teachable and come to understand!

The parable of The Hidden Treasure depicts a person who is not seeking a treasure and probably doesn't realize there is a treasure to be found, but he discovers it.

> *Again, the kingdom of heaven is like treasure hidden in a field, which a man found and hid; and for joy over it he goes and sells all that he has and buys that field.* (Matthew 13:44-46)

The next parable is the Pearl of Great Price. It seems to repeat the previous parable, but not exactly. This person knows the treasure he seeks: beautiful pearls. He already has value for the thing he seeks.

> *Again, the kingdom of heaven is like a merchant seeking beautiful pearls, who, when he had found one pearl of great price, went and sold all that he had and bought it.* (Matthew 13:35-46)

In one parable, a person who was not looking for a treasure found it; in the other parable, a person knew there was a treasure and was looking for it.

Both of these parables convey a common message. Whether you know what you are seeking or whether you stumble upon it, there is one essential attitudinal requirement: **you must want it more than you want anything else!** The men in both of these parables gladly sold all they had to purchase the treasure they found. Those who will not lay down their life in pursuit of the life God promises **never find it.**

For the better part of two thousand years, the church has primarily used negative, fear-based motivation. The only positive motivation (treasure) they offered was heaven after we die. That is an incredible motivation for those who have already tasted the goodness of God for themselves. They are eager to be with the Lord for eternity. But for those who do not know God, it's like preaching in a different language than the hearer speaks, hoping they will come to understand it… they rarely do!

If we intend to overcome two thousand years of negative fear-based preaching, we must be masters at pointing people to the treasure. Our message needs to be based on the Gospel: what Jesus did on the Cross, in the grave, and through the resurrection (1 Corinthians 15:1-4). It is these three components that open their eyes to the deep love of God. It also shows them that every aspect of life without God has been reconciled by what Jesus did. This makes it easy to trust Him. But we must walk the ultimate path. We must treat them with the love and goodness God shows us. Thereby, they do experience some degree of heaven on Earth. This taste of the treasure causes the hearers to open their hearts to the reality of the treasure that can become theirs: heaven on earth!

Discover Your Divine Prescriptions

- Take time to ponder what God spoke to you in this chapter.
- Ask Him, "In light of what I'm seeing, what are you speaking to me?"
- Then, "How do I apply what I'm seeing to my life?"
- Regardless of How I personally feel about what you're showing me, "You are my Lord. I am willing to follow your leadership."
- I am willing for you to bring me to the place of trusting and applying everything you speak to me."

29. Everything is Made New

In Christ, everything is new but is based on truth that has existed since before the foundation of the World!

When we see or hear the word "new," we always assume that it means either different or something that has never existed before now. However, in the Greek New Testament, we see that there are different words translated as new. One word means new and different in the way we understand it in English. But the other word translated as new means renewed or made better; it refers to the quality of the object that is new, not how it fits into time. Recognizing this simple factor will make everything we believe about God new, not different. It will give us a fresh new insight into God, His ways, and intentions.

As a new believer, I would often hear people talk about the God of the Old Testament and the God of the New Testament; it sounded as if they were describing two different entities! I knew the Bible said that God never changes, so I knew I was either misunderstanding what was being said or they were misspeaking!

Unraveling this mystery significantly opened the entire Bible to me. It made all of my doctrine consistent from Genesis to Revelation. It dramatically expanded my understanding of the New Covenant and Jesus' finished work!

As we study the apostles' writings, we realize that every revelation of Jesus and His finished work was discussed, described, and foretold in the Old Testament. In fact, all of Jesus' claims about being the Messiah were direct quotes from the Old Testament. The first thing that spoke to me was that if I didn't know the Old Testament, I would never fully know who Jesus was.

What we call the Old Testament, the Apostles called Scripture. Nothing in their writings implied that Scripture was no longer true, relevant, or that it was done away with.

The first confusion about this is in the English word "testament." The word testament would be better translated as covenant. In context, this word literally means disposition, covenant, or contract.[36] It is the Old Covenant that has faded away, i.e., been done away, not the Scripture. Paul's revelation and understanding of the New Covenant was based on the Old Testament Scriptures.

> **OUR IGNORANCE OF SCRIPTURE LEADS TO MOST OF OUR MISINTERPRETATIONS OF THE NEW TESTAMENT AND OUR LACK OF UNDERSTANDING OF THE NEW COVENANT!**

Our ignorance of Scripture leads to most of our misinterpretations of the New Testament and our lack of understanding of the New Covenant! The problem with the Old Testament has never been what it teaches; it's the veil over our hearts that affects our understanding, i.e., the way we read and interpret it! *"But their minds were blinded. For until this day the same veil remains unlifted **in the reading** of the Old Testament, because the veil is **taken away in Christ**."* (2 Corinthians 3:14)

Modern Christianity has sought to resolve our ignorance of the Old Testament (Scripture) by unwittingly claiming it has been abolished. But as

---

36 The Complete Word Study Dictionary: New Testament © 1992 by AMG International, Inc. Revised Edition, 1993

we previously discovered, it's actually the Old Covenant that has been abolished, not the Scripture.

The solution that resolves all our conflict is whether or not we read it with Christ as the lens through which we see and interpret what we read.

The aforementioned Scripture says the veil that clouded their understanding is lifted in Christ. It does not imply that being born again automatically removes the veil. The veil is lifted when we consider Christ to be the Rosetta Stone. For centuries, archaeologists were unable to translate ancient hieroglyphics until a stone was discovered that had the same message written in Greek and hieroglyphics. Since they were able to translate Greek, this gave them the key to translating a language that, up until then, no one could decipher.

Jesus is our Rosetta Stone. He is the basis for interpreting and understanding every Scripture in both the Old and New Testaments!

Jesus made it clear that He did not come to abolish the law and the prophets (Matthew 5:17). Instead, He came to fulfill them and bring them to their ultimate goal or purpose.[37] God's purpose did not change between the Old and New Testaments. The Law had its ultimate goal in the New Covenant. It was the tutor that would bring us to the place where we would realize our need for a Savior. It also provided perfect insight into the mind of God.

To help us understand the importance of this concept as something being new without the old being done away with. Let's look at the words of both Jesus and the Apostle John to discover how this can be.

In John 13:34-35, Jesus said:

> *A new commandment I give to you, that you love one another; as I have loved you, that you also love one another. By this all will know that you are My disciples, if you have love for one another.*

Actually, this is not a new (different) commandment. Jesus later pointed out that this is an old commandment. Leviticus 19:18, *"...you shall love*

---

[37] To perfect, consummate. to make complete in every particular; to render perfect: to carry through to the end, to accomplish, carry out,.to carry into effect, bring to realization, realize. Thayer's Greek Lexicon, Electronic Database. Copyright © 2000, 2003, 2006 by Biblesoft, Inc. All rights reserved.

your neighbor as yourself." So, was Jesus mistaken? No! The understanding comes by properly translating the word "new."[38] Not new as different, but new as in quality and freshness.

This is made even clearer by the words of the Apostle John.

> *Brethren, I write no new commandment to you, but an old **commandment which you have had from the beginning**. The old commandment is the word which you heard from the beginning. Again, **a new commandment** I write to you, which thing is true **in Him and in you**, because the **darkness is passing away, and the true light is already shining**.* (1 John 2:7-8)

Because of the translation issues, when we read this, we can get a little confused. "Is this a new commandment or not?"

This is not the first time this commandment has been given. God's intention was the same when it was first spoken as it was when John wrote it! God didn't change, and His intention didn't change. The original commandment was not done away with because it was in the "Old Testament." However, we could never understand this commandment the way God intended until we saw it put into practice by the Lord Jesus.

Through Christ's life, teaching, death, burial, and resurrection, the true light is shining on the word of God. In Him, we see God's original intentions in all He said. The freshness of this commandment is not that he was speaking it for the first time; it is the way we understand it when we interpret its meaning and application through what we see in Christ!

This particular Greek word for new is used many times. Here are a few instances.

- New Testament, 1 Corinthians 11:25
- New Creation, 2 Corinthians 5:17
- The New Man, Ephesians 4:24

---

38   New (especially in freshness: (Biblesoft's New Exhaustive Strong's Numbers and Concordance with Expanded Greek-Hebrew Dictionary. Copyright © 1994, 2003, 2006, 2010 Biblesoft, Inc. and International Bible Translators, Inc.) Qualitatively new, as contrasted with néos (3501), temporally new.
The Complete Word Study Dictionary: New Testament © 1992 by AMG International, Inc. Revised Edition, 1993

Everything is Made New

- Renew, 2 Corinthians 4:16, Ephesians 4:23, Titus 3:5
- New Covenant, Hebrews 8:8
- New Heavens and New Earth, 2 Peter 3:13
- New Commandment, 1 John 2:7-8

God didn't change the Old Covenant. He made it new and better in Christ, but it still had the same motives and intentions as the Old Covenant. He didn't change the commandments; He gave them a freshness in Christ that superseded the legalistic interpretations of the past. As new creations, we don't cease to be who we were, but we are made new. None of Jesus' commandments differed from anything in the law; they were made new and fresh because we could now see their true purpose and intention in Jesus.

Pop theology would have us believe that Jesus abolished the law and commandments and lowered the bar for love, righteousness, and godliness. However, Jesus did not lower the bar—he raised it! He made that clear in Matthew 5:20. *"Unless your righteousness exceeds the righteousness of the scribes and Pharisees, you will by no means enter the kingdom of heaven."*

> POP THEOLOGY WOULD HAVE US BELIEVE THAT JESUS ABOLISHED THE LAW AND COMMANDMENTS AND LOWERED THE BAR FOR LOVE, RIGHTEOUSNESS, AND GODLINESS.

We now know that He fulfilled the righteous requirements of the law perfectly. We have exchanged our sin for His righteousness.

Nothing in the Old Testament has been canceled, but it has been fulfilled in Christ, and we are in Him. He provides us with a righteousness far exceeding that of the Scribes and Pharisees. Plus, we have His grace that enables us to live and walk in His righteousness.

This is why we can choose to live in the Kingdom of Heaven and have the power to do so! It is a work He has done for us. He didn't do away with anything. He simply did what we could not do and gave it to us as a gift!

We realize that everything in the Old Testament is made new in Him. If we believe that, it is our responsibility to renew our minds, to see, understand, interpret, and apply all the Scriptures from our position in Him! Our first consideration for interpreting and applying any Scripture should be to ask, "What did this look like in Jesus' life, ministry, death, burial, and resurrection?

Renewing the mind occurs when we hear the word of the Kingdom of Heaven (seed) and prayerfully consider, reflect, study, meditate, pray, and listen to the Holy Spirit (the measure we meet) teach us what this looks like in real life. When we nurture the seed, we open our hearts to understand. The Holy Spirit can then teach us that all of God's word is still true, applicable, and essential.

One of the first functions of the heart is to establish our identity through what we believe. Planting and nurturing the seed until it bears fruit is how we move from the legal position of a new identity to the living experience of a new identity!

*"Therefore, if anyone is in Christ, he is a **new creation**; old things have passed away; behold, **all things have become new.**"* (2 Corinthians 5:17)

Discover Your Divine Prescriptions

- Take time to ponder what God spoke to you in this chapter.

- Ask Him, "In light of what I'm seeing, what are you speaking to me?"

- Then, "How do I apply what I'm seeing to my life?"

- Regardless of How I personally feel about what you're showing me, "You are my Lord. I am willing to follow your leadership."

- I am willing for you to bring me to the place of trusting and applying everything you speak to me."

30. A Way of Life

It's the things we do every day that define and direct our lives, not the things we do occasionally!

When you apply the *Immutable Law of the Seed* as a way of life, you will experience the greatest transformation you have ever imagined. You are now armed with the "know-how" employed by God to create all things that exist. Since this is how God created the entire physical world we now understand what Jesus meant when He said all things are possible to him who believes. By operating the same principles God employed to create all things, you enter into a dimension where nothing is beyond your reach.

Here's the question before you.

Will I make this way of life or just information that I never use?

If I want to be able to change my entire life, using this truth must be a way of life. As a way of life, this will require diligence and consistency, but that doesn't mean it will be hard!

Keep the following in mind!

Don't make this hard or mystical. No one needs to explain this to you beyond what you already know. All you need to do is put it into action.

> *For this commandment which I command you today is not too mysterious for you, nor is it far off. It is not in heaven, that you should say, 'Who will ascend into heaven for us and bring it to us, that we may hear it and do it?' Nor is it beyond the sea, that you should say, 'Who will go over the sea for us and bring it to us, that we may hear it and do it?' But the word is very near you, in your mouth and in your heart, that you may do it.* (Deuteronomy 30:11-14)

Anything else you desire to know about the *Law of The Seed*, you will discover as you put it into practice.

This is not new information. This is taught in the Scriptures and modeled by the way Jesus understood and taught the Scriptures. It may, however, be new and fresh in the way you read, understand, and apply it! As you seek to walk this out as a way of life, consider just a few ways that the *Immutable Law of the Seed* may enhance the truth you have known and applied for decades.

Faith

This will open a new insight and consistency in your walk of faith!

Many of the things we have done to build faith may be greatly enhanced when we realize we don't need to get more faith; we simply need to use our faith differently.

Instead of attempting to gain more faith, we can now remain at peace, realizing we all have a measure of faith. (That's a great starting place.) Since we do have faith in Jesus, expand your faith to include what Jesus taught.

Jesus said the way of bearing fruit occurs when we consider, reflect on, ponder, study, and meditate on the Word we hear. Allow the Holy Spirit to teach you, and the Word will eventually produce fruit!

Doubt and Unbelief

Instead of judging ourselves for doubt and unbelief, we may realize that after believing, we have continued to plant thorns in the garden of our hearts by the things we think, imagine, and talk about. It is the thorns choking the Word that we believed in the beginning! Our lack of faith isn't in the Word but a failure to apply the Word the way Jesus taught.

Confession

In the early days of the Charismatic and Word of Faith Movements, we were taught the power of confession. Unfortunately, some believers assumed that confession was something we did to move God. Now we realize that confession is a wonderful tool unless we use it with the wrong motive. Confession does not move God, but it does affect our hearts.

Now we realize that confession can be a powerful way of nurturing the seed we have planted in our hearts, which facilitates the production of fruit!

Giving

While giving is a form of sowing, it is not a seed that grows in our hearts. The seed that will grow in your heart is generosity. If you learn what the Bible says about generosity and choose it as a way of life, you can plant those seeds in your heart and then nurture them until they bear fruit.

Transformation

Any character trait you desire is as simple as sowing the seed in your heart. Meditating and experiencing yourself, living and enjoying the character you have chosen, and in due season, your heart, with the help of the Holy Spirit, will produce the desired trait in my life!

Growing in grace

When Jesus said, *"All things are possible, to him who believes,"* it must have been quite a shock to the listener. That had to sound out of the reach of their faith.

As new covenant believers, we know the secrets of faith and grace! The word grace comes from the Greek "charis." Charis has extensive meanings. It is far more than simply being gracious and kind. Paul used the word in a way that referred to God working in him to make him able to fulfill his calling and live in righteousness. After reviewing several language books, the compiled interpretations are "a power, ability, strength, and capacity that works from the heart and comes by unmerited favor." In 1 Corinthians 15:10, Paul said, by the grace of God, I am what I am. Grace is the power that transforms us from a sin nature to a righteous nature. It is our source for the ability, strength, and capacity to do and be all God says we can do and be in Jesus!

When you read or hear the promises of God, you can fulfill them all by simply applying the Law of The Seed.

Since everything God does in our lives is a work of faith and grace, there's no Bible promise that we can't experience! All things are possible for us because we not only believe in Jesus but also believe in and follow His teachings concerning the *Immutable Law of the Seed*!

Every area of Your Life

I encourage you to find ways to apply the *Immutable Law of the Seed* to everything you seek to do and be in Christ!

Discover Your Divine Prescription

- Take some time to consider areas of your walk with God where you plan to apply the *Immutable Law of the Seed*.
- Search and find Scriptures that you will write and use as seeds.
- Spend time nurturing them in your heart through prayer, study, pondering, considering, reflecting, and meditating.
- See and experience the Scriptural outcome you desire, i.e., see and experience the end from the beginning!

About the Author

In 1972, Dr. James B. Richards accepted Christ and answered the call to ministry. His dramatic conversion and passion for helping hurting people launched him onto the streets of Huntsville, Alabama. Early on in his mission to reach teenagers and drug abusers, his ministry quickly grew into a home church that eventually led to the birth of Impact Ministries.

With doctorates in theology, human behavior and alternative medicine, and an honorary doctorate in world evangelism, Jim has received certified training as a detox specialist and drug counselor. His uncompromising, yet positive, approach to the gospel strengthens, instructs and challenges people to new levels of victory, power, and service. Jim's extensive experience in working with substance abuse, codependency, and other social/emotional issues has led him to pioneer effective, creative, Bible-based approaches to ministry that meet the needs of today's world.

Most importantly, Jim believes that people need to be made whole by experiencing God's unconditional love. His messages are simple, practical, and powerful. His passion is to change the way the world sees God so that people can experience a relationship with Him through Jesus.

To learn more about Dr. Jim Richards and Impact Ministries visit: https://impactministries.com/

www.ingramcontent.com/pod-product-compliance
Lightning Source LLC
Chambersburg PA
CBHW060532100426
42743CB00009B/1499